MITCHELL PARK BRANCH

Palo Alto City Library

WHAT TEENAGERS WANT TO KNOW ABOUT SEX

QUESTIONS AND ANSWERS

WHAT TEENAGERS WANT TO KNOW ABOUT SEX

QUESTIONS AND ANSWERS

BY BOSTON CHILDREN'S HOSPITAL

Robert P. Masland, Jr., M.D.
MEDICAL EDITOR

David Estridge
EXECUTIVE EDITOR

LITTLE, BROWN AND COMPANY
BOSTON   TORONTO

FIRST EDITION

Library of Congress Cataloging-in-Publication Data
What teenagers want to know about sex: questions and
answers/by Boston Children's Hospital: Robert P. Masland,
Jr., medical editor, David Estridge, executive editor. — 1st
ed.
    p.   cm.
  Includes index.
  Summary: Provides information, in a question-and-
answer format, on all aspects of male and female sexuality
including puberty, hygiene and health, menstruation,
conception, sexual identity, contraception, variations in
sexual behavior, rape, sexual abuse, and other related
topics.
  ISBN 0-316-25063-5 : $16.95
  1. Sex instruction for teenagers — Miscellanea. 2.
Teenagers — Sexual behavior — Miscellanea — Juvenile
literature. 3. Sexual ethics — Miscellanea — Juvenile
literature. [1. Sex instruction for youth — Miscellanea.
2. Sexual ethics — Miscellanea. 3. Questions and
Answers.] I. Masland, Robert P. II. Estridge, David. III.
Children's Hospital (Boston, Mass.)
HQ35.W42   1988
613.9'5'088055 — dc19   87-36680
                                        CIP
                                        AC

10 9 8 7 6 5 4 3 2

RRD-VA

*Published simultaneously in Canada
by Little, Brown & Company (Canada) Limited*

PRINTED IN THE UNITED STATES OF AMERICA

CONTENTS

About Robert P. Masland, Jr., M.D.

Dr. Robert P. Masland, Jr., is the Chief of the Division of Adolescent and Young Adult Medicine at Children's Hospital. Dr. Masland's experience as a personal physician for thousands of teenagers gives him the ideal background to understand the issues that young people face.

For more than thirty years, he has worked with adolescents and their families, listening to their questions and concerns. He is able to respond in a manner that is truthful, clear, reassuring, and nonjudgmental, even to complicated or difficult issues.

Dr. Masland organizes and leads student seminars on human development and sexuality. His frequent interaction with sensitive, bright young people has kept him in close touch with their priorities, feelings, and needs.

An Associate Professor of Pediatrics at Harvard Medical School, Dr. Masland is widely regarded by colleagues and students as one of the most capable and skilled teachers at the medical school and at Children's.

About Boston Children's Hospital

Boston Children's Hospital is the largest pediatric health care institution in the United States and the world's largest pediatric research center. Founded in 1869 as a twenty-bed hospital for children, it is now an internationally renowned center for comprehensive pediatric health care. Approximately one-third of its patients are adolescents and young adults.

Children's is the primary pediatric teaching hospital of the Harvard Medical School, where most of its senior physicians hold faculty appointments.

Editorial Board

A WORD ABOUT WHAT TO EXPECT

This book is for you and about you.

It tells how girls and boys grow and mature into young women and young men. It describes the physical and emotional changes that occur in the teenage years, one of the most interesting, eventful times of life.

The questions and answers that follow cover a wide range of issues dealing with human growth, development, emotions, and feelings. They explore in detail the usually slow, sometimes tumultuous process of becoming an adult.

Preteens and teenagers representing a broad spectrum of races, religions, socioeconomic levels, and geographic regions actually created this book. Members of the Health Information Department of Boston Children's Hospital visited many middle schools and high schools and asked students to share their questions, concerns, and uncertainties. Department members also wrote to teachers and sex educators across the country to learn what were the most common questions and confusing issues concerning the teenage years.

Everyone responded superbly, speaking honestly and in remarkable detail. In fact, the questions were so far-reaching and so helpful that it seemed natural to let them form the backbone of this book.

The questions were arranged by general topics, and the chapters are organized using these areas of interest. This format allows you to use the book in several ways:

- You can read it straight through from beginning to end as a resource and reference work on human reproduction, sexuality, and personal relationships.

- You can use it as a handy reference to browse through, a chapter or two at a time, or to track down information and answers to specific questions.

- You can check with it from time to time to see how the natural sequences of physical and emotional development usually occur and to find out what to expect.

Truthful information about human development and sexuality is important in order to understand the physical and emotional changes that occur during adolescence and then to make sensible decisions. Parents, teachers, and other trusted adults help shape your ideas, beliefs, and values, but you are the one in control of your mind, your body, and your actions.

ROBERT P. MASLAND, JR., M.D.

WHAT TEENAGERS WANT TO KNOW ABOUT SEX

QUESTIONS AND ANSWERS

CHAPTER 1

PUBERTY: A TIME OF CHANGE

What is puberty?

Puberty (PYOU-ber-tee) is the time of rapid physical development when sexual reproduction first becomes possible. In other words, this is the time when a male becomes physically able to impregnate a female, and a female is physically able to get pregnant and have a baby. Sometimes people use "puberty" and "adolescence" as if they meant the same thing, but it is more accurate to use the term "puberty" when talking about the many *physical* changes that occur during the preteenage and teenage years.

What is adolescence?

"Adolescence" refers to the *emotional* and *social* changes of the teenage years. Adolescence usually occurs about two years after puberty begins and reflects the impact of the physical changes of puberty. Emotional experiences deepen. Females and males mature, take on increased responsibilities, and develop greater expectations about themselves and others. At the same time, social changes play a major role in adolescence, as male and female activities become more varied and individual.

How does the shape of the body change during the teen years?

Generally speaking, females' lower bodies and males' upper bodies grow wider. Perhaps the most noticeable change for females during this period is breast development. At about the same time, hips and thighs increase in size as the female hormone estrogen (ESS-troh-jin) causes the body to lay down additional fat cells. The pelvic area also widens, to allow the passage of a baby at birth.

Boys usually develop broader shoulders, with more muscle in the upper body, but remain slim through the hips and thighs. This is because the increase in the male hormone testosterone (tes-TOSS-ta-rone) stimulates muscle development.

When visualizing the outline of a "typical" boy's shape, you see an upside-down triangle with the wide part at the shoulders and the sides narrowing down toward the waist and hips. For the girl, the triangle is right side up with the wide part at the pelvic area and the sides narrowing somewhat through the upper body. Of course, there are many variations on these basic shapes. For example, if a young woman is a rower, she probably has large shoulders and greater upper body development. If she is a runner or high-jumper, her legs and thighs probably will be quite muscular and lean. Some boys during puberty seem to be pear-shaped. Much of a person's physical development depends on how other members of his or her family are built and what physical traits have been inherited.

When and where does body hair start to grow?

Body hair refers to pubic (PEW-bik) and underarm hair for both males and females and facial hair for males. Pubic hair is the thick, wiry hair that grows in the genital areas (the areas in which the sex organs are located) in both males and females. Generally, pubic hair is darker than hair that grows on the head. For females, pubic hair begins to grow as early as age eight; boys' pubic hair starts a little later, perhaps beginning at age ten. Girls who do not have any pubic hair by fourteen and boys who do not have any pubic hair by fifteen should check with a doctor. Usually, the "problem" is only a delayed beginning of puberty.

Hair under the arms comes a bit later, so that if pubic hair begins for a girl at age ten, her underarm hair may begin around the age of twelve. Boys usually begin to develop underarm and facial hair about two years after their pubic hair has begun. Most boys at first rarely have enough facial hair to require daily shaving. Usually, facial hair begins on the upper lip and sideburns. Perhaps a few hairs will sprout on the chin, but usually not many. Young girls may have some facial hair, again in the same places as boys —

on the upper lip and sideburns. This may begin sometime around the first menstrual period, but it usually does not continue to grow and rarely becomes unsightly.

Why do some teenagers develop a small amount of hair and others develop a great deal?

This difference usually is the result of family characteristics, called heredity. A boy whose father has a heavy beard that started early in puberty can expect to have early, heavy hair growth himself. If a mother has facial hair, her daughter also may have some.

At what age do a female's breasts begin to develop?

Breasts begin to develop as early as eight years of age and as late as fourteen. About half of developing females will have breast development and pubic hair begin at the same time, while the rest will have one or the other begin first. If breasts begin to develop first, then pubic hair usually develops within a year, and vice versa.

Why do females wear bras?

A bra is worn mainly for support. The breast has connective tissue and structures resembling ligaments that naturally support it. As a female grows older, the connective tissue and structures that suspend the breast become more relaxed and unable to support it firmly. Wearing a bra is more comfortable than going braless for most women. Also, younger women who have somewhat larger breasts may feel self-conscious about their size and may prefer to wear a bra to reduce the appearance of having large breasts.

Wearing a bra, even before there is any clear physical need, is a sign of the passage into adolescence. Some females who are eager to develop may wear padded bras to suggest that their breast development is under way.

When does a young man's voice change?

As pubic hair comes in, the testicles grow, secreting the male hormone testosterone, which, in turn, causes a change in the voice. The vocal cords lengthen so that the voice becomes deeper. Voice change usually occurs when a boy experiences a growth spurt in height — perhaps two or three inches over six months. That happens between age thirteen and sixteen years, or about halfway through adolescent sexual growth. It is possible, however, for some boys to have deep voices before puberty because of heredity. Other boys may have a relatively high-pitched voice that may not become deeper even after puberty.

Males and females can, to some extent, control the quality and tone of their voices through training, but the physical changes that the vocal cords undergo in puberty limit the extent of that voice control. A boy who sang soprano before adolescence, for example, will not remain a soprano during and after adolescence. His voice will deepen, and he may sing tenor, baritone, or bass.

Do your senses or facial features change during puberty?

Other physical changes that sometimes occur during the years of puberty — changes in eyesight or hearing, for example — usually have no direct connection with puberty. They are not caused by sex hormones and should not be considered part of sexual maturation. You might imagine that changes in the shape of the nose and ears and in the amount and texture of hair are part of sexual development because they happen at roughly the same time. Some of these changes surely are hereditary, while others may be the result of normal growth. Certainly, many hormones that are not involved in sexual development are playing their own roles in the body.

What are hormones, and how do they work during puberty?

Hormones are complex chemicals that certain organs (such as the ovaries or testicles) or glands (such as the thyroid, pituitary, or adrenal) produce and send into the bloodstream. These hormones travel to other organs and glands that require a special hormone to perform a particular function.

Among the many hormones the body produces are those that are known as male and female hormones. Males have mostly male hormones and a bit of female, and females have mostly female hormones with a small amount of male. That's normal.

Male hormones, such as testosterone, and female hormones, such as estrogen and progesterone (pro-JESS-ta-rone), trigger breast and genital organ development and growth of pubic hair. There are also some hormones that stimulate a target area in the body to affect its activity, such as one of the pituitary hormones that stimulates the ovaries to produce an egg, a process called ovulation. (See Chapter 7, "Menstruation," and Chapter 10, "Conception and Pregnancy.")

Each hormone has certain properties that may protect the body. For example, older males are more likely than females to have heart attacks and blood vessel diseases, perhaps because the female hormone estrogen protects the body against those problems. Males have a slight protection against heart disease because they naturally produce just a tiny amount of estrogen. But if men were to take estrogen pills to gain extra protection against heart attacks, this amount of estrogen could cause their breasts to enlarge, and they could gain extra weight.

How do I know if my body is normal?

Unless you recently have had a physical examination, you will not know if your body is normal for your age. And even if your doctor says you are on schedule, you may be made uncertain by comparing your development with that of your friends. Generally speaking, most females are self-conscious about the development, size, and appearance of their breasts. Most males are concerned about penis size and length. Whether pubic and underarm hair is developing on time may worry both males and females. It takes time for everyone to develop, and some people develop more rapidly than others.

CHAPTER 2

THOUGHTS, FEELINGS, AND CONCERNS OF TEENAGERS

How can I get someone to like me?

If you are sensitive to the talents, interests, and concerns of others — what they like to do and when — and if you have the ability to project or convey that sensitivity to another person, you will find that others will like you. If you are self-centered, if all you can do is talk about what you like, want, and are interested in, you probably are not going to have too many people interested in you — in fact, they may find you boring. You should be willing to listen and not overwhelm your companion with your accomplishments or opinions.

How can I tell if I'm in love?

Young people's feelings can be extremely intense and important. It is difficult to pinpoint what the signs of love might be for a particular person. The peaks and valleys seem to be of enormous significance, and feelings can change quickly. The key could be (and often is) physical attraction, or a mutual interest, such as music, sports, or a hobby. People can be attracted to each other because they find it easy to communicate. To try to point out in any meaningful way the differences between love and attraction is probably foolish. Trying to do so assumes an ability to read the minds — and hearts — of those who feel they are in love.

How can I tell if someone is really in love with me?

There are two crucial requirements for a positive relationship. The first is availability — that is, closeness in location or time. And the second is personality — that is, how well and naturally you get along together. If you see a great deal of a person because you share classes or interests, you naturally are going to have more opportunities to learn about each other. If you find someone who is congenial, easy to talk to, interested in you, kind, sympathetic, and giving, you soon realize how much fun it can be to spend time with that person.

After finding that you like each other and want to spend time together, you both have to decide whether you want to move any further in the relationship. If both of you are truly interested in each other, you may be able to compromise on some of your ideas, and then perhaps each can satisfy part of what the other wants and needs.

How can I tell if my feelings or if others' feelings are love or just sexual attraction?

Because teenagers usually possess such a high level of sexual awareness, it is extremely difficult to decide whether what you are feeling is love. The emphasis often falls on how attractive a person is physically and how much you are attracted and impressed by someone's appearance. What may feel like love can be, in fact, a very powerful, even magnetic, sexual attraction. And, for many teenagers, only after they are no longer together will they realize that their strong feelings were physical attraction or passion, and not love, after all.

For adults, although love and passion may go hand in hand, love usually grows into a more important, stronger feeling than passion. Love is the more stable force. Passion comes and goes, but love goes on and on.

How can I become sexually attractive?

Contrary to what advertising may claim, being sexually attractive is not confined to having a beautiful body or well-developed muscles. Personal qualities do attract admirers and will make a boy or a girl want to know you better — to call you a friend. For example, both sexes are interested in someone whom they can talk to easily about almost any subject. Making oneself attractive is never just a matter of physical appearance. It is important to think of yourself as an attractive person and to make every conscious effort to show yourself as someone who can relate honestly, directly, and thoughtfully to others.

You might also project your independence and individuality, so that you are not merely patterning yourself after the most popular guy or the best-looking girl. Similarly, it is not always a good idea to be associated with only one type of person or be a member of just one group — the jocks, the brains, the beauty queens, or the party people. In order to be taken seriously by someone you consider desirable, you need to be your own best version of yourself. This is not an easy balance to strike. Sometimes you will find it a bit lonely when you are not sure just where you fit in and who can be counted on as a friend. It is some comfort to know that *everyone* feels uncertain some of the time, even the leaders and "coolest" kids in the class.

How do I know if my sexual feelings are normal?

You *won't* know if your sexual feelings are normal because at the beginning you have little or nothing to compare them with except stories of your friends or members of your family.

Most teenagers worry about whether their sexual feelings may be weird, crazy, or sick. As strange as it may sound, it is normal to be concerned about all sorts of sexual feelings. There is so much happening to the adolescent male or female body that it is difficult to keep up with all of the changes and developments. As long as these feelings do not interfere with a teenager's usual activities or cause strange behavior, nothing need be done. If a teenager feels especially uncomfortable, it sometimes is helpful to talk things over with a doctor or perhaps a counselor.

How does a person decide what values to have about sex: parents' values, religious values, friends' values?

No one decides to have certain values. By the time you are a teenager, many of your family's values already have been transmitted — that is, learned and accepted. Values come from your parents, other members of your family, your religious and ethnic background, and your close friends.

Choices about sexuality are conditioned by your background and training. You have to consider how your decisions will affect those closest to you, your personal values, your religious values, and your long-term goals, such as education and career.

In addition, unconscious motives and feelings will play a part in decisions you make about what to do and what not to do sexually. For example, how you feel about your parents and brothers and sisters, about your role models, about authority and rules, will affect what you eventually decide is right for you to do — or not do — sexually. As you know, many of your deepest, strongest feelings have been part of you since earliest childhood.

Who's in control of my body — me or my parents?

You are in control of your body, and you have the responsibility for its care and protection. Your parents, of course, have a stake in the consequences of your actions. Consequences refer not only to the possibility of an unplanned pregnancy but also to the short- and long-term emotional complications of relationships. It always takes time and experience to learn how to handle powerful feelings. Parents can offer valuable suggestions and guidance based upon their own experiences. Ultimately, of course, you are in charge of your body, what you do with it, and how you care for it.

How can I say no to having sex and still be liked, and how do I deal with peer pressure?

It is possible to say no and still be accepted, even admired, by your friends, especially those who truly care for you. It becomes easier as teenagers move into their middle and late teen years to resist the pressures and temptations of those who say, "Everybody's doing it." The ability and self-confidence to say no are important not only in regard to sex but also to the use of alcohol, tobacco, and drugs of all kinds.

How can I say no without losing the person I care for?

First of all, a person who truly cares about you should not pressure you into doing something against your will. Losing the person you care for, however, may be necessary if it means sticking to your principles and sense of personal values. The ability to say no and follow through on that decision can be most valuable in the long run even if it means ending a relationship. Learning to live with a decision is one of the keys to growing up.

How do I answer, "You would if you loved me"?

This familiar, well-worn approach, almost always used by a male to influence a female's reluctance to yield to sexual advances, can make her feel immature and inadequate unless she realizes that she always is in control of her own body and her life. Having the courage to simply say "No" can be an important milestone.

Is it wrong to tease someone sexually?

It usually depends upon the situation, the people involved, and the kind of teasing. Males and females often tease one another. Teasing usually is not right or wrong, it just makes things difficult, occasionally uncomfortable, for the other person. However, if the teasing does harm to the other person, then it is out of bounds.

How can I figure out how far I really want to go?

There is no such thing as an emotional road map to provide direction and instruction about specific situations. It is impossible to tell someone in advance how to set arbitrary limits. Most people just know when they should stop.

An individual's sense of when to say no has to do with personal and family values, the messages learned through school and religious teachings, the influences and experiences of friends, and the emotional intensity of the relationship. At the very least, a young woman should consider whether she wants to risk getting pregnant, and a young man should consider whether he wants to risk getting a girl pregnant, and both should be concerned about sexually transmitted diseases.

Do sex and love go hand in hand?

Sex and love may very well go hand in hand if there is mutual respect and commitment between the two people involved.

Two people who are in love certainly may want to include sex as part of their relationship; however, it is not necessary. Sex without love is often criticized as tempting but possibly risky, especially for someone young and inexperienced who could, perhaps, be taken advantage of by an older, more experienced person.

At what age should I have sex?

There cannot be a general "right" chronological age to have

sexual intercourse (the mating of a male and a female). This has to be a matter of individual judgment and preference.

How old are most young women and men when they first have sexual intercourse?

According to statistics from the Alan Guttmacher Institute, by nineteen years of age about 70 percent of females and about 80 percent of males have had intercourse at least once. If you are a male or a female who has not had intercourse by the age when statistics indicate that many people your age already have, you should not feel pressured to have your first sexual encounter. It is better to have sex when you are ready and in a situation comfortable to you. Until you feel ready, it is correct to say no. No matter what anyone says to persuade you, you don't have to have sex to be grown up.

Is it OK to have premarital sex?

Deciding whether it is all right for two people to have intercourse depends on many factors, such as personal values and religion. If two people are in love, if they are mature and realistic, and if they have made a commitment to each other, then an intimate relationship may be a natural extension of their friendship. If two people share a real commitment, including an understanding of the consequences and responsibilities of a sexual relationship, then they may be ready to engage in a responsible act. Whether it is OK for a particular couple to have premarital sex is obviously an issue that no one can comment on without knowing the two people quite well.

If there is sensitivity to each other's feelings, if contraceptives (measures taken to prevent pregnancy) are used, and if both partners are free of sexually transmitted diseases, sexual intercourse may be a valid, responsible, and mutually agreeable decision.

Have society's attitudes changed about virginity? If so, why?

Yes, attitudes have changed. Whether it is desirable to remain a virgin until marriage is a value judgment that cannot be made in the abstract. The effect of the women's rights movement and the increasingly equal nature of our society have provided greater acceptance of independent activities by women, including sex. In addition, women are marrying at a later age than in past generations, and they may feel comfortable being involved in a sexual relationship without the commitment of marriage.

Is virginity undesirable now?

It is probably not accurate or fair to say that virginity ever is "undesirable." Among some young teenagers who are sexually active, virginity may be regarded as old-fashioned, but that often is a way of trying to justify their own actions.

Is sex important?

Sex can be an important, effective way of expressing affection, tenderness, love, and emotional attachment. It is not the only way of doing so, but few other expressions of human feeling can match the intensity of caring sexual behavior.

Is sex essential?

Sex is not something that one should think of as Nirvana, paradise, or the ultimate fulfillment. Sex obviously is essential to the continuation of the species, and it is a healthy part of a lasting personal relationship; but it usually does not occupy a crucial role throughout one's life, especially among older adults.

What is a normal reaction to sexual intercourse — enjoyment, passion, guilt, fear, dislike, disgust, or nothing?

Don't expect fireworks! People hope for enjoyment, pleasure, or excitement, and these can happen if the commitment to the other person and the relationship are genuine. Intercourse is only one part of the total relationship. In time, physical passion is possible, especially after two people have gotten to know each other and have discovered what gives them pleasure. Guilt, fear, dislike, disgust, or no feeling can be the result if one or both partners' priority is sheer physical sensation.

Is it wrong to have sex just for enjoyment, without a commitment?

It is impossible to make a value judgment about whether having sex for sheer pleasure is right or wrong without referring to a specific couple. It may be a fulfilling, positive experience for some people in certain situations, but not for others. This is a question that has to be decided by the people directly involved, based upon their values, beliefs, feelings, education, and family background.

Are one-night stands OK?

Although I usually don't voice a judgment concerning matters of private choice, in this case I have a strong opinion. One-night stands are not good, positive experiences for teenagers. By their very nature — brief, impersonal, possibly impulsive — one-night stands do not provide the right setting or enough time to learn about your own needs and feelings or those of your partner. In addition, one-night stands increase the risk of contracting a sexually transmitted disease. Discovering your own sexuality and becoming familiar and relaxed with someone else's requires sharing much more than a few hours in bed together.

Is sleeping with more than one person considered promiscuity?

It depends on how many more than one we are talking about. If it is two, it would be difficult to consider that promiscuity. Once the number gets up to three, four, five, and so on, this clearly falls into the territory of promiscuity — which means that a person is not very selective about his or her sexual encounters. People who have multiple partners also run the risk of becoming the subjects of rumors and gossip. More important, sexually transmitted diseases — including acquired immune deficiency syndrome (AIDS) — should give people considerable reason for concern if they are involved with multiple partners.

Once I've had intercourse, will I automatically want to sleep with the next person I like?

No. Your feelings may be similar to those aroused by your previous partner, but that does not mean you have lost judgment or your sense of self-control. You are not on "cruise control," so to speak, once you have had a single sexual encounter. You are always free to put on the brakes whenever you please!

Is intercourse habit-forming?

No, but during the teen and young adult years when opportunities for intercourse can be plentiful, some males and females may assume or even fear that it can be habit-forming. In addition, there is the old refrain that too much sex too soon can make people "slaves of passion." That myth could have something to do with a fear that sex can become an addiction, an impulse beyond the self-control of a male or female. It is a mistake to underestimate the strength of the feelings and passions of young men and women going through adolescence. At the same time, it is worth remembering that even the most demanding and consuming emotions can be controlled and channeled.

What makes a good sex life?

Sexual relations alone will never make a good sex life. A couple must have several shared interests in addition to their physical and sexual attraction to each other if they want to sustain a meaningful, satisfying relationship. Once two people have found a number of common interests and activities, they can always decide on what kind of physical relationship they desire. For teenagers, in particular, their physical relationship need not include sexual intercourse. If the partners truly care about each other's needs and emotions, they will discuss in detail and agree upon what kinds of intimacy can satisfy and give each pleasure. In an ongoing relationship, partners' needs and feelings change and develop, and how they physically express them changes as well.

Does birth control destroy the spontaneity of sex?

No, but it certainly does go a long way toward avoiding pregnancy! Some young females assume that by taking a birth-control pill, they are announcing their readiness or availability for sexual activity. But, in reality, that is just not so. For the male, not using a condom during intercourse in order to assure spontaneity is irresponsible. (See Chapter 11, "Contraception.")

Why is sex education such an embarrassing subject for parents and teachers?

Parents and teachers are often uncomfortable with sex education because they believe that young people will become sexually active after receiving the information. If sexual activity occurs, parents and teachers may feel responsible or guilty.

Parents may recall their own sexual feelings and encounters

when they were adolescents. Mothers of this generation generally are more comfortable discussing sexual matters with their daughters than fathers are talking with their sons. Mothers seem to be better informed in talking about menstruation, intercourse, birth control, abortion, and related subjects with their daughters. Many fathers are uncomfortable discussing any kind of sexuality, and some expect their sons to learn the facts of life from friends, reading, or "on the street." So it still is the exception rather than the rule that young males can get reliable, timely, and emotionally neutral information on sexuality from their parents.

If there is a sex education course in school with teachers who are well informed and at ease with the subject, you should take advantage of this opportunity. If those classes provide chances for discussions, they could lead to helpful discussions at home, assuming your parents are familiar with the course and its materials.

Do people know more than they used to about sex?

It is my impression that they do. There is more accurate information about sex available today than a generation ago. As a result, children and adolescents know more at an earlier age.

Another way of answering this question is to point to the increase in knowledge about human reproductive biology and the many fine research projects going on all over the world that give us greater knowledge and deeper understanding of sexuality. One result of this increase in information and knowledge is that sexuality now is much less a taboo subject than it was twenty years ago, and more people of all ages feel comfortable discussing it.

What is the double standard?

The double standard regarding sexual behavior has to do with a male's freedom to do certain things without criticism, punishment, or social isolation, while a female who does the same things is subjected to any or all three reactions. For example, a male who engages in sexual intercourse before marriage may be praised as a "he-man" or macho and aggressive, while a female who does the same thing may be criticized as "loose," "fast," or "easy." That is the double standard in its most obvious and unfair form.

Although the so-called sexual revolution of the 1960s and 1970s has somewhat reduced this glaring inconsistency, it is still true that many females in our society are judged by a higher standard of sexual morality. Theoretically, females have the same sexual freedom and choice as men, but they are not expected to be as assertive or aggressive as males in most social or professional situations, and this attitude surely can affect a young woman's sense of self-worth.

It is also true that traditional sex roles — men out competing in the world, women running the home and raising the children — are much less conventional now than they were just a generation ago. Traditional sex roles tend to restrict both males and females, overlooking their individual strengths and needs. Men often want to be involved in running the home and raising children, while women often find careers rewarding. The important thing is for people to be comfortable with themselves.

CHAPTER 3

HUMAN REPRODUCTIVE SYSTEMS: WHAT THEY ARE, WHAT THEY DO

What does the term "reproductive system" refer to?

The reproductive system is a group of related organs in the human body that have two main functions: performing various kinds of sexual activity, and conceiving and giving birth.

Does "reproductive system" mean the same thing as "sex organs"?

Generally speaking, the terms "reproductive system" and "sex organs" have quite similar meanings. However, the reproductive system includes the sex organs plus other related areas as well, such as the female breast.

What does "genital" mean?

"Genital" as an adjective can refer to either the sex organs or the reproductive system. Used as a noun, "genitals" usually means the male and female external sex organs, the visible and partly visible ones.

THE FEMALE BODY

What are the major parts of the female reproductive system?

In the upper part of the body, there are the breasts. Located in the abdomen are the ovaries and a pair of closely associated organs, the fallopian tubes. Just below these is the uterus (or womb); the entryway to the uterus is called the cervix. In the lowest part of the abdomen there are the vagina and the organs connected with it, the vulva, labia, clitoris, and hymen. (See Figure 1.)

What sexual function do breasts have for the female?

Breasts are organs that provide nourishment for babies. Females may find that fondling the breast causes sexual arousal, and males may be sexually attracted to breasts.

What is the normal breast size for females?

A single "normal" breast size does not exist. There are, in fact, many sizes and shapes of breasts within the range of what is considered normal, depending upon the body size and build of an individual. Breast size is like so many other things in life — you want to have something that is just right. "Just right," however, is often a matter of personal opinion.

In our culture there continues to be great fascination with the size of the female breast. Many males and females, with plenty of help from the media, advertising, and the fashion world, focus on the size and shape of the breast as a sexual object.

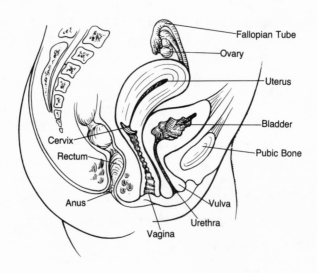

FIGURE 1. The Female Reproductive System.

Can a female's breasts be of different sizes?

Most breasts are not absolutely identical, but any difference, however minor, usually is obvious only to the female herself. It is quite rare to have an extraordinary difference in breast size.

Why are some women's nipples larger or darker than others'?

Women's nipples differ in shape, size, and color because of heredity. It has nothing to do with a disorder. Pregnancy and breast-feeding can temporarily enlarge and alter the nipples.

Is it normal to have nipples that turn inward?

Inward-turning nipples are not abnormal, but just a variation from normal development. This may occur on one breast or both. These nipples may be persuaded to face outward through special exercises. A female may want to do these exercises if she is preparing to nurse an infant. For teenagers, as the breast slowly enlarges, the nipples may begin to turn outward, but this does not always occur. During sexual arousal, inverted nipples may turn outward.

Why do nipples get hard and dry during sexual arousal?

Nipples get hard during sexual excitement because they contain erectile tissue ("erectile" means capable of becoming hard or rigid). Both male and female nipples have this special type of tissue. Nipples also can get hard without sexual excitement; the rubbing of a close-fitting garment or feeling chilly, for example, can trigger the erectile tissue. There is no physical reason for a female's nipples to become dry during sexual arousal. Pregnant or nursing women, however, may secrete some milk during sexual excitement.

What are the openings in the female genital area?

There are three separate openings, each with a different function. From front to back there are the urethra (you-REE-thra) for eliminating urine from the bladder; the vagina (va-JEYE-na) for eliminating the menstrual flow from the uterus, for having sexual intercourse, and for giving birth; and the anus, (A-ness) for eliminating solid waste.

What are the ovaries?

Women have two ovaries, which serve as the "factories" for producing eggs. Each ovary is about the size and shape of an almond. At birth, every female normally has about 400,000 eggs in her ovaries, waiting to mature.

After a female reaches sexual maturity, her ovaries begin to release the eggs at the rate of one per month. This is called ovulation (AWV-you-lay-shun). The release is triggered by the monthly secretion of a particular hormone. Each month as many as six eggs may ripen, but only one is usually released by the ovaries. The unreleased ripened eggs are absorbed by the body. If two or more are released and more than one is fertilized, a multiple birth will occur.

If the egg is not fertilized, it is discharged from the body as part of the menstrual flow (see Chapter 7, "Menstruation").

What are the fallopian tubes?

The fallopian (fell-LOW-pee-yun) tubes are channels that lead from the ovaries to the uterus. The egg travels down these channels and implants itself into the lining of the uterus. The fallopian tubes project out from the top of the uterus, one on each side. They are about four inches long and narrower than a drinking straw. At the top, each fallopian tube has a tiny, fringelike projection of tissue, called a fimbria (FIM-bree-a), which reaches out and wraps around each ovary.

How are fallopian tubes involved in the journey of an egg?

At the time of ovulation each month, the fimbria at the end of one of the fallopian tubes receives the egg just as it is released by one of the ovaries. On the inside of the fallopian tubes, microscopic hairlike fibers help propel the egg down toward the uterus. The egg cannot travel down the fallopian tube without this push, which resembles a miniature conveyor belt moving the egg along.

Fertilization (when sperm from the male unites with the egg) almost always takes place inside the fallopian tubes. Very rarely, fertilization occurs outside the fallopian tubes, and then usually in the uterus.

What is the uterus, and is it the same as the womb?

The uterus (YOU-tur-us), another name for the womb (WOOM), is a muscular organ normally about the size and shape of a small pear. It usually tilts forward a bit toward the front of the abdomen. During pregnancy, the uterus is "home" and a source of nourishment for the developing baby. It expands greatly in size to meet the demands of the growing child.

The smooth muscle of the uterus is very strong and thick, but it works differently from the muscles in our arms and legs (called skeletal muscle) because it is controlled automatically by the nervous system. During childbirth, for example, the uterus contracts and pushes the baby into the vagina. The uterus also contracts slightly during the menstrual period to help remove its lining. (See Chapter 7, "Menstruation.")

What is the cervix?

The cervix (SER-vix) is the outlet of the uterus. It extends down into the top of the vagina. The cervix is the entrance to the uterus and fallopian tubes, and sperm travel up through the cervix after sexual intercourse. The cervix also provides the exit from the uterus for menstrual flow.

What is the vagina?

The vagina is perhaps the best-known and most frequently discussed of all the female sexual organs. The vagina has three main uses: it is the opening for sexual intercourse, the passage for the menstrual flow to be carried out of the body, and the birth canal. If you visualize a short, narrow balloon before it is inflated, with its very flexible sides pressed against each other, that is pretty close to the shape of the vagina inside the female body. The smooth, soft sides (or walls) of the vagina can expand or contract easily.

Does the size of the vagina differ from female to female, and does the size make a difference?

The size of the vagina varies from female to female, depending somewhat on her age. The preadolescent female obviously has a less developed vagina, which is shorter than an adult's. After a girl begins puberty, however, her vagina lengthens somewhat and its sides become more moist. When puberty is complete, vaginal size changes very little and is just about the same in most adult females.

The size of the vagina matters little since it stretches easily to accept the erect penis during intercourse and stretches greatly during childbirth. Following childbirth, however, some females have a more relaxed vagina as a result of stretching of the vaginal walls.

What is the vulva?

The word "vulva" means "covering" and refers to the covering (or protection) of the female reproductive outlet — the entire genital area of the vagina and urethra. The vulva includes the most visible features of the female genital area — the pubic hair; the outer lips (or labia); and the mons (MONZ), the pad of soft, fatty tissue that covers the pubic bone in the lowest part of the abdomen, just above where the legs come together.

What are the labia?

The word "labia" (LAY-be-a) means "lips" and refers to the visible part of the vaginal area. There are the large, or major, lips, which are quite apparent in the preadolescent female, and the small, or minor, lips. In the female who has not had children, the small lips can be seen only if the large lips are separated. The small lips are very thin folds of tissue, and after a woman has had children, these inner lips become easier to see. The labia are sometimes called the entryway to the vagina.

What is the clitoris?

The clitoris (KLIT-a-riss), located in the front of the vulva area, looks simply like a small round bump, but beneath the skin there follows an attached short, slender shaft. The size of the clitoris varies slightly in adults; a half inch is about average. The clitoris is a major source of a female's sexual sensitivity because of the extensive network of nerves at its tip. Tissue in the clitoris can become erect, causing it to enlarge slightly when a female is sexually excited. The clitoris probably exists exclusively to give sexual pleasure.

What is the hymen?

The hymen is a thin layer of tissue that stretches across the vagina about an inch or so inside. Often it is just a ring of tissue, not really a full screen, that narrows the vagina. And it is possible to have a hymen that obstructs or screens the vagina only slightly or not at all. The hymen has no known function.

Does every female have a hymen?

The hymen is present in all females, and it can have different shapes. Slang terms for the hymen include "cherry" and "maidenhead."

What causes the hymen to break?

The hymen can break during the first experience with sexual intercourse. It was once believed that *only* a female's first sexual intercourse would break her hymen, but this is not true. It is impossible to tell whether a female is a virgin simply by checking for an unbroken hymen. In fact, the hymens of some young females break naturally without intercourse during normal growth and development. Certain forms of exercise, such as cycling or horseback riding, are said to be responsible for breaking the hymen.

There may be some minor bleeding and slight pain when the hymen breaks or tears. Sometimes, however, the hymen simply stretches gradually and naturally, so there will be no bleeding or pain during the first intercourse.

In most females the hymen is not completely closed, so using tampons in most cases will not tear the hymen. A female with a nearly closed hymen, however, may have trouble inserting a tampon into the vagina. Females who have experienced trouble inserting tampons or who may be concerned about pain or bleeding with first intercourse can have a doctor enlarge the opening in the hymen.

Can the hymen present a problem when a female begins to menstruate?

In rare cases, the hymen completely covers the vagina, so blood is trapped inside the vagina and uterus, causing them to enlarge. This condition can lead to other problems. This problem, however, can be easily corrected by a doctor, who carefully slits the tissue of the hymen to relieve the blockage.

THE MALE BODY

What are the major parts of the male reproductive system?

The major parts of the male reproductive system are the penis, the testicles (or testes), the scrotum, the seminal vesicles, the vas deferens, and the prostate gland. (See Figure 2.)

What is the penis?

It is the male sexual organ, located at the bottom of the abdomen. Shaped like a tube, the penis (PEE-ness) consists of two parts: the rounded tip, called the head (or glans), and the shaft, which becomes hard during erections. The penis contains special cells that enlarge during sexual excitement.

The penis has several different functions. The penis contains the urethra, the channel that carries urine out of the body. During sexual excitement, when the penis becomes erect, semen (SEE-

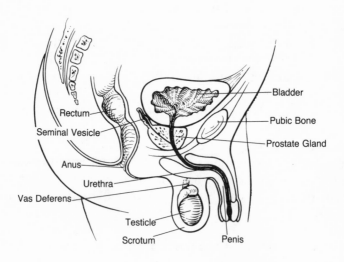

FIGURE 2. The Male Reproductive System.

min, a fluid containing sperm, the male sex cells) is released through the urethra in the process called ejaculation. The penis also is the source of great sexual pleasure when stimulated by touching, rubbing, or other sexual activity.

What is the normal size of a penis when it is not erect?

Our society loves comparisons and seems obsessed with size. In the same way that we tend to focus endlessly on breast size, there is a fascination with penis size. The average nonerect penis is about three inches long.

How much larger does a penis get during an erection?

When the penis is erect, a male who has a somewhat larger relaxed penis really does not get much larger than someone who has a smaller penis. The usual length for the erect penis is 5½ to 6½ inches. A female can accommodate a longer — or smaller or wider or slimmer — erect penis in her vagina without any problem.

Does penis size affect sexual satisfaction?

Penis size has nothing at all to do with sexual satisfaction — except perhaps in some people's minds. If the sexual relationship is loving and caring, the size of the penis itself makes no difference.

What difference does penis size make generally?

Concern about the size of a male's penis invariably is a reflection of personal anxiety. Penis size has nothing to do with performance or satisfaction. Boys who are delayed in their sexual development and those who are overweight often are self-conscious in a locker room where their genitals can be seen. These boys may be ridiculed by their peers for having what appears to be a small penis. On the other hand, boys who are well-endowed, or "well-hung," receive praise for being so "macho." But, in fact, these differences are meaningless, since penis size has nothing to do with sexual function or sexual pleasure.

If sperm and urine come out of the same opening in a man's penis, does that mean a man can urinate when he ejaculates?

Sperm and urine do come out of the same opening, but not at the same time. It is physically impossible for a male to urinate during ejaculation because at that time the exit from the bladder to the urethra is closed. A male who sees a slightly yellowish tinge to the semen may think that urine has leaked into his ejaculation. The yellow, however, is probably normal, because semen varies in color from milky white to very pale yellow.

What are the testicles?

Testicles are the male sex glands, sometimes called gonads or "balls," which create sperm in sexually mature males in response to special hormones. Each testicle consists of tiny tubes that look like tightly coiled threads. These tubes are contained in tiny compartments within each testicle. When males grow during the early years of adolescence, the coiled tubes grow as sperm are produced, making the testicles larger in the process.

Is it normal for a male to have one testicle lower and larger than the other?

Yes, the left testicle is usually lower. The testicles are never exactly the same size — another example of the many differences between the right and left side of the body. If there is significant difference in size — if one testicle is very small and the other is much larger — a doctor should be consulted.

Are both testicles needed for reproduction?

Only one testicle is needed for reproduction. In fact, if a male loses a testicle or is born with only one functioning testicle, the one healthy testicle will increase its normal production of sperm by as much as 25 percent.

What is the scrotum?

The scrotum (SKRO-tum) is the flexible bag of skin that holds the testicles.

Why do the testicles sometimes pull up next to the body?

There are muscles inside the scrotum that are sensitive to heat and cold. The testicles must be kept at just the right temperature in order for sperm to be produced. That temperature is a little lower than body temperature, so the testicles normally hang away from the body. They are suspended inside the scrotum by a stretchy cord resembling a ligament, which can contract and pull the testicle toward the body. This action, which is the result of a special muscle called the cremaster muscle, occurs automatically when the testicles are exposed to cold temperatures; when a male is frightened; when there is harm to the body, particularly to the genital area; and when a male is sexually excited.

What are sperm?

Sperm are the male sex cells necessary for fertilization of eggs. Sperm, which are so tiny that a microscope is needed to see them, are produced in the testicles.

What is semen?

Semen is the fluid ejaculated from the penis during the peak of sexual excitement. Semen contains sperm, seminiferous fluid, and fluid from the Cowper's glands, two pea-sized structures near the urethra and in front of the prostate gland.

What happens to the body if sperm are not released?

Nothing happens if the sperm are not released. Sperm are continuously being generated by the testicles and stored in the seminal vesicles. If there is no ejaculation within a week or so, sperm are simply absorbed by the body.

What is the clear, sticky fluid that comes from the tip of the penis when a male first gets an erection?

It is a type of lubricating fluid thought to make intercourse easier. Two very small structures called the Cowper's glands secrete this fluid. The rest of the fluid produced by these glands goes into the semen.

That tiny bit of fluid may contain enough sperm to cause a pregnancy. Even a small amount of this fluid can make a female pregnant by a male who inserts and withdraws his penis without actually ejaculating.

What are the vas deferens?

The vas deferens (VAS DEF-er-enz) are two slim tubes, sometimes called sperm ducts. Each delivers sperm from one testicle to the seminal vesicles for storage until ejaculation.

What are the seminal vesicles and what is seminal, or seminiferous, fluid?

The seminal vesicles (VESS-i-culs) are two small coiled-up tubes located behind the scrotum, near the prostate gland. Each produces fluid for semen (seminal, or seminiferous, fluid) that is stored in the vesicle with sperm that have made the trip from the testicles in the vas deferens. About 60 to 70 percent of the fluid in semen is from the seminal vesicles.

What is the prostate gland?

The prostate (PROSS-tate) gland is a small organ located behind the scrotum. It surrounds the urethra at a point near the bladder. The prostate supplies 30 to 40 percent of the fluid in the semen.

What is an erection?

An erection (often called a "hard-on") is an enlargement and hardening of the penis as a result of increased blood flow into the organ. The increased blood flow occurs as a result of physical or emotional stimulation, and this prepares the penis for the possibility of sexual intercourse.

Is it necessary to have an erection to have intercourse?

An erect penis is essential for sexual intercourse. A male must have an erection so that he can insert his penis into the vagina.

What exactly are "wet dreams" and why do they occur?

"Wet dreams" are ejaculations that young adolescent males have while sleeping. These ejaculations, sometimes called nocturnal emissions, may be stimulated by sexually explicit or erotic dreams.

CHAPTER 4

WHAT IS SEXUALITY?

What is sexuality?

Humans are sexual beings. Sexuality refers to:

- how males and females differ from and resemble each other physically, psychologically, and in terms of behavior;

- the activities, feelings, and attitudes associated with reproduction; and

- how males and females interact in pairs and in groups.

To put it in more down-to-earth language, sexuality is how a person feels about and expresses his or her particular sexual nature and characteristics.

Being sexual starts with the many changes of puberty during adolescence and continues throughout all of adult life. Rather than limiting sexuality to the period when someone is beginning sexual activity, we need to think of a more adequate definition that combines the way a person develops attitudes and feelings about being male or female; the way he or she relates physically and emotionally to members of the same and opposite sex; and how comfortable the person is with being male or female.

How does sexuality differ from men to women?

We all know the basic physical differences between male and female bodies. It is doubtful, however, that the internal sense of sexuality — how each sex understands itself and expresses its particular sexual nature — is essentially different between male and female. True, males and females send different sexual cues or signals — some verbal, some physical. And those signals, naturally, vary according to whether the audience is male or female. However, it is difficult to identify or describe how it feels inside to be a male or a female except by referring to specific kinds of activity.

What does it mean to be masculine or feminine?

Masculinity and femininity in the basic sense are determined at birth by inheritance (chromosomes) and then by development of the appropriate genital organs. However, being masculine or being feminine is not solely determined by genes. Masculine and feminine are subjective concepts, based on individual as well as social values and beliefs. It would be possible, for example, to have a clearly masculine body and yet have what some people might consider to be feminine characteristics of behavior. That kind of "inconsistency" should not be considered unusual or "weird." Variations make us all, males and females, interesting and distinctive. Even though we often hear the expressions, "He's all man!" or "She's a real woman!" there probably is no totally masculine man or totally feminine woman. (See Chapter 15, "Sexual Identity.")

Is sexual behavior instinctive?

Instinct is an inborn tendency to act in a way characteristic of a species — how we expect humans or kangaroos or fish to behave, for example. Some species display sexual behavior patterns and rituals that are instinctive. For a human being, becoming sexually aroused may feel instinctive and unplanned, but the decision to have sex and then the timing and performance of the sexual act require some planning, experience, and self-awareness. Only humans are capable of that particular kind of thinking ahead and planning.

Is the so-called sex drive psychological or physical?

Instinctive sexual behavior is sometimes referred to as the "sex drive" or the "libido" (li-BEE-doe). For human beings, however, we really should think of the sex drive as a complicated mixture of emotional and physical factors and influences. For any one person it is almost impossible to sort out which factors are dominant.

What causes the sex drive?

Sometimes the sex drive in adolescents — their preoccupation with sexual thoughts and desires — is attributed to the influence of excessive amounts of hormones. Short of careful examination and testing, it is difficult to sort out what is purely physical and what comes from the stimulation of peer pressure and trying to fit in and act like "everyone else."

Why is the sex drive stronger in some people than in others?

All people are different, and some people naturally enjoy sexual activities more than others. It's simply a matter of preference, just as some people like going to the movies or going out to dinner more than others. If we tried to scientifically study a "sexual athlete" — a person who is supposed to have a strong sex drive, or libido — we would undoubtedly have a very difficult time finding *any* physical or biological basis for this. Unfortunately, entertainment and the media glamorize males and females who are supposed to have extraordinary libidos. Such people often behave in a way that promotes their self-image, especially if it is intended to attract attention.

Does the sex drive differ from males to females?

The sex drive probably does not differ from male to female in the sense that one sex is generally more interested in sexual activities than the other. Both sexes seem equally interested in and available for sexual activity, and the historical social disapproval of a female's having a healthy interest in sex has greatly relaxed.

What is frigidity?

The term "frigid" usually refers to a female who is supposed to be cold, unresponsive, or hostile toward sexual advances. Both the term and the thinking behind it frequently are distorted and misleading, especially since a young man may use the term as a way of degrading a female he may not like or getting back at one who has rejected him. The word "frigid" is neither helpful nor accurate. Describing a condition, attitude, or feeling is always preferable to using labels.

It is true, however, that some females feel uncomfortable with men — just as some males may not feel at ease with women. In intimate situations certain females may not be able to respond naturally or warmly to a male's affection. Some women who would like to be able to respond more positively may find it helpful to discuss concerns with a physician, psychologist, or sex therapist.

Is it normal to have fantasies and sex dreams, and what age group has them most often?

It is quite normal to have fantasies and sex dreams. Males and females of all ages have them. Fantasizing is a natural way to enhance sexual experiences.

What causes sexual arousal?

Let's talk first about attraction. Males and females are attracted to each other in many obvious and subtle ways. It may be looks, dress, talk, or just how a person relates to someone of the opposite sex. There may be no physical contact at all. Human beings also may become attracted and then physically excited, or "horny," by physical or mental stimulation. It can happen when two people get to know each other or it may be something that happens in someone's head just by thinking or fantasizing about a person. However, it is a mistake to think of sexual arousal as the trigger for a process of escalating stimulation and excitement that always leads to sexual intercourse.

Why do I become sexually aroused? Why does my heart beat faster?

You become aroused because after entering puberty hormonal activity increases. Development of your nervous system becomes more complex and responsive to sexual stimuli. These factors make it possible for you to become aroused. Many of your involuntary body functions, including heartbeat, increase in rate or speed.

Is it normal to get sexually excited just by looking at someone you think is attractive?

Visual stimulation is an important part of the whole sexual experience. It is natural to become aroused by looking at a person you find attractive. It also is natural to be attracted to certain body parts. For example, some males find breasts irresistible. Others may have a preference for legs, hips, hands, arms, or hair. Some females find male chests attractive. Others may be attracted to shoulders, legs, or general physique.

What are erogenous zones?

The erogenous (a-RAH-jen-us) zones are the parts or regions of the body most directly connected with sexual excitement. The word "erogenous" means "producing sexual desire." For the female, the erogenous zones include the breasts and the genital organs, especially the vaginal area and the clitoris. For the male, they usually focus upon the genital organs, particularly the penis. However, the mouth, ears, legs, feet, shoulders, or any other part of the body can be erogenous. Those areas are sensitive not only because of the number of nerve endings there but because of the psychological anticipation that builds when each partner knows what the other likes.

What is an orgasm?

For a male, orgasm (OR-gaz-em), or sexual climax, is ejaculation. The erect penis ejects semen in several vigorous spurts or squirts. Orgasms can occur during sexual intercourse, masturbation, or "wet dreams." For a female, orgasm is the climactic contraction of the vaginal muscles and uterus. It may occur as the result of stimulation of the clitoris, vagina, or both. It usually happens more gradually than male orgasm. The expression "to come" means to have an orgasm.

What does orgasm feel like?

The actual pleasurable feeling during orgasm varies greatly. Orgasms can be powerful and exciting: some males say that orgasm feels as if they are being taken over by a powerful, physical force. Others say that it is a release from the growing physical and emotional tension preceding it — like the breaking of a wave.

Females often describe an orgasm as a tremendous, pleasurable explosion deep within that is powerfully exhilarating and then incredibly relaxing.

Does a man's orgasm feel different from a woman's?

It is not possible to compare male and female orgasms because each orgasm is a physical-emotional event with special characteristics for each person.

Why are some orgasms stronger than others?

For the male, the strength of an orgasm often is related to the number of times ejaculation has occurred in a specific period of time. General physical health can also play a role. Orgasm may be diminished or even impossible for someone who is ill or has a chronic disease, is poorly nourished, or is taking certain medications or drugs, especially alcohol. If a male has repeated orgasms in a relatively brief time — say, an hour — then the later ones usually are less vigorous and generally shorter in duration.

For the female, some orgasms are stronger than others because of variations in physical and emotional factors, each of which contributes something to the overall feeling. The strength of successive orgasms for a female may have more to do with the emotional intensity (passion) than the physical stimulation of the sexual act, regardless of how vigorous her partner may be.

Are orgasms emotional or physical or both?

Females and males experience orgasms physically and emotionally. Males have more physical evidence of orgasm because of the ejaculation. Because a female orgasm does not produce an obvious physical sign, it has been thought that perhaps females experience a greater emotional orgasm. That is sheer guesswork, however, and probably not true. Males experience intense emotion during orgasm, but this emotion may be expressed in a different way from that of females.

How often can a woman or a man have an orgasm?

Some females are capable of having multiple orgasms during a single sexual encounter. For a male, one orgasm per sexual encounter is the norm.

Do men have more orgasms than women?

Men tend to be more consistent at achieving orgasm than women and therefore probably have more orgasms. Depending upon age, some younger men are capable of having a second erection and orgasm within an hour or so of the first one. As men grow older, they become less able to have successive erections and ejaculations.

Can a person suffer any damage if he or she has a great sexual excitement but doesn't have intercourse or doesn't have an orgasm?

There is no physical harm to any of the sexual organs if sexual excitement does not bring about orgasm.

Must sex be a part of a satisfying relationship?

A male or a female can feel at ease in the company of someone who is attractive physically, emotionally, and intellectually. This mutual attraction can be satisfying and comfortable when two people are together even if sex is not part of their relationship.

In a marriage, does sex become less exciting; become necessary to keep the marriage healthy and happy; cause adjustment problems?

Whether sex becomes less exciting always depends to some degree on the personalities of those involved. For some couples, sex may become fairly routine and less exciting, but other couples may find sex becomes more exciting as the partners become comfortable and familiar with each other.

Sex is not absolutely necessary to keep all marriages happy and healthy. Some people do not consider sexual relations essential. Some couples may be well adjusted and enjoy each other's company without needing the stimulation of sex. Other couples, however, find that sex is an important part of the closeness and intimacy of marriage.

Newly married couples may find that they can adjust to each other more happily if they go for counseling about a sexual problem. A physician may be able to talk with them or provide a referral to a counselor, perhaps a licensed sex therapist.

Adjustment problems may appear to be related to sexual difficulties, but this need not be so. Often people who are having a variety of interpersonal problems may focus upon their sexual differences to the exclusion of more pressing issues. It is also true that after many years together some couples who are satisfied with their sexual relations are totally dissatisfied with the rest of their marriage.

How old are most people when they stop having sex?

People who are physically sound and feel so inclined may continue sexual activities throughout their lives, certainly into the seventies. That means that there is no particular time when people stop having sex because some never do. Maintaining sexual relations is strictly an individual matter.

Who can a teenager talk to about sexual hang-ups or problems of sexual adjustment or identity?

A teenager should feel free to discuss sexuality with family members, a trusted adult, or a physician. Local health clinics may also be able to offer suggestions about where to get sound advice and information. It's always difficult to gather up the courage to say "I don't know" or "This is really bothering me." But remember that there are many people who can make a world of difference by talking straight with young people about their doubts, worries, and uncertainties. (See Chapter 15, "Sexual Identity.")

CHAPTER 5

MALE SEXUALITY

At what age is a male capable of having sex?

A male is physically able to have sex when he can maintain an erection and then ejaculate. This usually occurs between the ages of thirteen and sixteen. The first ejaculation may be the result of either a "wet dream" (an orgasm that happens accidentally during sleep) or masturbation (self-stimulation). (See Chapter 9, "Sexual Activities.")

If young men don't mature as fast as young women, how come so many seem so interested in sex so soon?

That's not really hard to figure out. We find adult sexuality portrayed and glorified in our culture — in newspapers and magazines, on the television and in movies, in popular music and videos, in clothes and sports gear. One message clearly is that in order to be a "real male" a boy must begin to think and behave heterosexually (attracted to the opposite sex) as early in life as possible.

Young males — preteens and young teenagers — probably are not as fascinated by sexuality as they sometimes seem to be or as the media like to show them. We often see a sophistication in teenagers' conversation, dress, and sexual experimentation that makes many of them uncomfortable.

The fact that a male has a penis probably is partly responsible for boys' early preoccupation with sexuality. After all, that visible sexual organ does become erect, is involved in masturbation, and becomes a focus for fantasies and dreams. (See Chapter 9, "Sexual Activities.")

When do males reach the peak of their sexual drive?

Scientists have found that testosterone levels reach their peak in the late adolescent years, and this is when the male sex drive usually reaches its highest level. Sex drive, however, is always a subjective term, and what truly matters is how a particular male feels about engaging in sexual activity. Significantly, the decline in testosterone levels in later years is quite gradual, which means that the male sex drive, at least as measured by testosterone levels, remains essentially constant into the forties or fifties.

What causes an erection?

Erections occur in response to involuntary nerves, which cannot be consciously controlled, and are triggered physically or emotionally. Sexual excitement, emotional stimulation or fantasy, physical friction, masturbation, erotic thought or visual experiences, and even a full bladder pressing on the penis and prostate gland all can cause an erection.

What does an erection feel like?

There is no particular physical feeling or sensation associated with an erection, unless it occurs while a male is wearing tight underpants or clothing that causes pressure or friction on the erect penis. The feeling, of course, is psychological — one of excitement and anticipation. An erection that occurs while a male is naked may produce a sensation of fullness, heaviness, or tautness when the skin of the penis is pulled tight as a result of the increased volume of blood in the penis. Some males who do not achieve a climax — do not ejaculate — complain of pain or a feeling of congestion because of the lack of a hoped-for release. This pain may, in fact, exist more in the mind than in the penis.

How long can a man have an erection?

For some males an erection can last for up to an hour with prolonged stimulation, but usually it lasts much less time.

Can a man always have an erection when he wants to?

A man cannot always have an erection, and when he cannot that condition is called impotence. The condition can be temporary or long-term. Males are capable of repeated erections, but the older the male the longer it usually takes to achieve another one.

Erections sometimes can be very embarrassing and ill-timed, especially for adolescents. Erotic thoughts, the sight of a shapely female body, or tight-fitting pants can trigger an erection, even if the male wishes to avoid it. These spontaneous erections usually do not happen on conspicuously public occasions, such as while reciting in class, during a stage play, or while waiting for your burger in a fast food restaurant; but, as many young men discover, they can happen even there.

How can a man prevent himself from getting an erection?

There is no guaranteed method to avoid having an erection — not even wearing an athletic supporter as some males often recommend. Sometimes a male can deliberately divert his thoughts to something unpleasant or distracting as a way of causing the erection to relax, but that is not a foolproof technique.

Why do males sometimes wake up in the morning with an erection?

The primary cause for morning erections is a full bladder, which puts pressure on the prostate gland. The prostate then stimulates the nervous system, triggering increased blood flow to the penis. This type of erection has very little to do with sexual arousal and does not interfere with the ability to urinate.

What is an ejaculation, and how does it happen?

Ejaculation is the forceful release of semen from the erect penis. Semen, which is fluid from the prostate gland and seminal vesicles, contains sperm produced in the testicles. Semen is delivered into the urethra and then out of the penis through involuntary contractions. Ejaculation occurs at the peak of male sexual stimulation. Although a male may know when he is about to ejaculate, he has little control over his ejaculation.

Males who are fatigued, have been drinking alcohol, or are taking certain drugs or medications may have an erection but not ejaculation. Others who have recently ejaculated may not be able to ejaculate again until a certain period of time has elapsed. Rarely, a male may be unable to ejaculate after a prolonged erection and stimulation. Should this happen repeatedly, a male should consult a physician.

Is there a "normal" number of ejaculations per month, per hour, or per sexual encounter?

There is no normal number of ejaculations. It is an individual, private matter, and we should do everything possible to get away from playing the numbers game. Keeping score is a very poor substitute for valuing the quality of our emotional and sexual lives. The number of ejaculations a male is capable of per period of time or sexual encounter is meaningless except as a very superficial way of bragging.

Is it painful when a man ejaculates?

Ejaculation is not painful ordinarily, but it might be if a male has an underlying medical problem, such as an infection of the urethra or the prostate gland. The physical act of ejaculation is quite vigorous, especially for adolescents during puberty. At first the sensation may feel strange and out of control. If ejaculation seems somehow painful at first, that feeling becomes pleasurable quite soon.

Does an ejaculation sap a man's strength?

Ejaculation does not sap a male's strength. This idea is another bit of folklore without any truth. Directly following ejaculation a male may feel spent, but that has nothing to do with weakness. In addition, men often feel so relaxed after ejaculation that they fall asleep. This phase, however, usually passes quickly, especially for young males.

Does a man have an orgasm each time he ejaculates?

Ejaculation and orgasm are the same thing for men. At times, some males may not ejaculate a large amount of semen, but this usually is related to having had recent prior ejaculation(s) or to the existence of an underlying physical disorder, especially an infection.

If a male does not release sperm, does the buildup of excess sperm cause "blue balls"?

Sperm have nothing to do with "blue balls," a slang term referring to the color of the swollen blood vessels in the scrotum. These vessels swell during sexual arousal and activity. This is not harmful. A young male is most likely to complain of having blue balls after a female has purportedly denied him sexual satisfaction when he is sexually excited and does not have an ejaculation, or because there is no available partner.

Do all males have wet dreams?

All males have wet dreams. Although they are a sign of sexual maturity, young males sometimes are embarrassed because the semen ejaculated will stain pajamas and bed linen.

How often do males have wet dreams?

Wet dreams happen much more frequently during early and middle adolescence — perhaps once or twice a week — than later adolescence and adulthood. Young males who have a history of bed-wetting may be concerned by their first wet dreams, fearing that they are a recurrence of their problem. A male who finds himself in that situation should consult an adult male for reassurance that he is normal and that this is altogether different from bed-wetting.

What is premature ejaculation, and what causes it?

Premature ejaculation means that a male ejaculates, or "comes," before he enters his partner or very soon after penetration occurs. It can be embarrassing and upsetting for both partners, but especially for the male.

Premature ejaculation is common for a young male because he is aroused easily and often ejaculates quickly, sometimes even before he is aware of what is happening. Sexual anxiety or conflict may also be the cause of premature ejaculation for older males who find themselves in situations where they worry about performing sexually or where they feel uncertain whether their partner will be satisfied.

If a male ejaculates prematurely during his first two or three sexual encounters, he may find himself anticipating this problem each time he is aroused. This makes it difficult for him to have an unhurried ejaculation.

Is there anything that can be done to stop premature ejaculation?

If premature ejaculation occurs repeatedly and causes increasing anxiety or unhappiness for one or both partners, counseling often is helpful. A physician who is experienced in such problems and is a good counselor may be consulted. The individual (or both partners) may want a referral to a psychologist, psychiatrist, or sex therapist if the problem seems particularly difficult to deal with. Sex therapists may be able to prescribe specific emotional and physical techniques, including the "squeeze technique." The squeeze technique involves gently squeezing right under the tip of the penis just before the male has the sensation that he is about to ejaculate.

Is a male's sperm supply cut down if he jogs long distances and trains very hard?

It is possible that the level of the male sex hormone, testosterone, is not as high among highly trained male distance runners, but the reduction should not be significant nor should it have any noticeable effect on male sexual behavior. We do know that concerted, strenuous athletic training can reduce a woman's estrogen level, thereby affecting or even interrupting her menstrual cycle, but a negative training effect upon males seems unlikely; research may someday give us better information.

Do males lose their ability to have sex at a certain age?

Males do not lose their ability to have sex at a certain or specific age, although their ability to have frequent or repeated erections and ejaculations usually begins to decrease during the forties and fifties.

Do males ever lose the ability to reproduce?

Males remain fertile (able to produce an adequate amount of healthy sperm) and able to have sexual relations into their sixties. Because a man's sperm count will begin to decline, it is unlikely that a male past his mid-sixties or into his seventies will succeed in impregnating a woman. There are examples, however, of men who became fathers in their seventies. Such men obviously were fertile, able to achieve an erection, and able to have an ejaculation. At any age a male may temporarily or permanently lose his ability to have sexual relations because of illness or as a result of taking medicines that interfere with sexual performance, especially the ability to have an erection.

Is there a male counterpart to menopause?

"Menopause," the end of the reproductive phase of a woman's life, is a term that applies only to females. However, in midlife — the late forties and early fifties — when hormone levels are decreasing, some men may experience a psychological slowdown or depression that some doctors refer to as the "climacteric" or "midlife crisis." Sexual performance may decline, and depression, mild or severe, may develop. Difficulties with career, marriage, and family sometimes occur simultaneously. Habits such as alcohol or drug abuse may begin at that stage in a man's life. For a male, these generalized midlife changes occur over time and do not have a definite endpoint such as menopause in a woman's life (see Chapter 6, "Female Sexuality").

FEMALE SEXUALITY

What physical changes take place when a woman is sexually aroused?

When a person (male or female) blushes, either from excitement or embarrassment, blood rushes to the face. This is a form of flushing. When a female is sexually excited, there may be flushing of her skin, especially the face, chest, and breasts. Her nipples may become erect, and her breasts may enlarge very slightly. In addition, her vaginal secretions may increase, and she may feel a tingling sensation in her clitoris and vagina. These are all normal automatic physical changes that happen as the nervous system responds to hormones.

What causes wetness in the genital area when a female is sexually excited?

The wetness comes from the vagina itself. It is a mucous secretion from the tissue in the vaginal wall. Some lubricating mucus in the vagina is also secreted by small organs called Bartholin's glands. These secretions make intercourse easier and more pleasant for both the female and her partner.

A female cannot control the amount of these secretions or how long it takes for the lubrication to be felt. Some women become wet with very little sexual arousal, while others whose lubricating mucus comes in more slowly need a longer period of petting, or foreplay, before beginning intercourse (see Chapter 9, "Sexual Activities"). Some females feel dry regularly or occasionally and find intercourse uncomfortable unless they use a lubricant. Still others, when they are sexually excited, become excessively wet and, unfortunately, may feel self-conscious or embarrassed.

Do females experience anything that is similar to male ejaculation?

Obviously, females do not ejaculate at the peak of their orgasm as males do, but some females may have an extra surge of vaginal lubrication when the muscles of the vagina contract during orgasm.

When does a woman start having orgasms?

Even before reaching puberty, a young female may find that masturbation (self-stimulation of the clitoris) is satisfying and pleasurable. But she may not experience orgasm until well into middle to late adolescence.

How long does it take a woman to reach orgasm?

An orgasm can occur within a few minutes of direct sexual stimulation or it can take much longer. Again, achieving an orgasm is not a stopwatch kind of exercise — the quality of the experience is much more important than how long it takes. Achieving orgasm is highly individual, depending not only on the female and her emotional and physical makeup, but also on the time, place, and circumstances — that is, what is going on around her at the time. By concentrating on how quickly an orgasm occurs or how long it lasts, all the other vivid, important feelings can be missed.

What is the difference between vaginal and clitoral orgasm?

Some females may experience orgasm when the clitoris is stimulated, while others may experience orgasm when the vagina is stimulated. The intensity of the orgasm can vary depending upon which part of the body is most sensitive and responsive. For a female, the experience of having an orgasm can be pleasurable and satisfying regardless of how or where or by whom (with a partner or through masturbation) the orgasm is produced.

What does it mean if a woman never has an orgasm?

It really does not mean much at all. In our society, measuring degrees of sexual satisfaction or fulfillment by number and intensity of orgasms has become common. As a result, some females may worry about their sexual adequacy if they have not experienced an orgasm, either by themselves or with a partner. If a female does not have a physical problem, such as an anatomical abnormality or an illness, she should be able to experience an orgasm. If a female has an underlying emotional problem that needs to be better understood, she might want to talk with a physician, counselor, or sex therapist.

Do young women have wet dreams? If so, is any substance produced?

Females can have dreams containing sexual fantasies. In fact, some young women say that they awaken from such dreams sexually aroused, perhaps even in the middle of what feels like an orgasm. In such situations, there may be increased vaginal lubrication, but young women do not experience actual wet dreams.

At what age does a woman reach the peak of her sexual desire?

There is no known or certain age when a female reaches the height of sexual desire or ability to feel sexual passion. Some experts have identified that peak as thirty-five years of age, but there is no scientifically accurate way of determining that time for every — or any — particular female. Scientists have found that female hormone levels are generally highest around age thirty-five, but what truly matters in estimating sexual desire is how someone feels — what is going on in an individual's mind and emotions.

Does a female lose her ability to have sex at a certain age?

Absolutely not! Feelings about sex and interest in it may vary with age, but a female's ability to have sex remains unchanged. She is always able to have sex, assuming health, desire, and, of course, a suitable partner.

What is menopause, and when does it occur?

Menopause is that time of life when a female's menstrual cycle ceases (see Chapter 7, "Menstruation"). It means that a female has stopped ovulating because the amount of the hormone estrogen being produced is not large enough to produce a menstrual period. Menopause lasts anywhere from one year to five years.

Menopause occurs at different times for different females. It may occur at any time from the early forties to the early fifties. If the females in a particular family follow a pattern of having menopause in their mid-forties, the chances are good that a woman in that family reaching forty-five or forty-six will experience menopause herself. If a female has undergone surgery to remove her ovaries, or if the ovaries have been subjected to radiation and/or chemotherapy, then menopause would begin earlier.

What physical and psychological changes occur during menopause?

The menstrual period decreases in length until it stops altogether. When females begin to produce less estrogen, the physical changes that occur are connected with the aging process. Skin texture is less firm and moist, and skin elasticity decreases. Hair may become less luxurious and full. Additional facial hair may appear. The bones weaken because they lose calcium (osteoporosis). There may be occasional, unexpected heavy menstrual flows because of the occurrence of a surge of estrogen in the absence of progesterone to stop the bleeding.

Some women may experience what are called hot flashes, a feeling of sudden, intense warmth accompanied by sweating, which can be extremely uncomfortable. Hot flashes, which are often unpredictable and embarrassing, may be caused by a sudden surge of estrogen, the female sex hormone. This estrogen surge seems more pronounced because of the generally low levels of estrogen present in the body of a female who is nearing or going through menopause.

Women may experience the end of their childbearing years as a loss, and some may feel unhappy and depressed. Other women view menopause as a time when they can feel free and uninhibited about sexual activities because they do not have the fear of an unplanned pregnancy. Obviously, every female has her own individual feelings. It is difficult and inaccurate to link with menopause the wide variety of psychological changes that a woman goes through at that stage of her life. Menopause is just one of many changes that occur roughly at midlife.

Does menopause affect a woman's sexual performance?

Menopause does not affect a woman's sexual performance, but it may affect her interest in sex and sexual activities. Attitudes differ about the beginning of signs of menopause. A woman may not feel as positive about her body and attractiveness during menopause and afterward, and, as a result, may feel less eager for sexual contact. Other women may welcome the end of the childbearing years and find themselves more interested in sexual activities.

Does a female stop ovulating when her periods decrease in length?

Ovulation may continue even when periods do not last the customary number of days or even if periods occur irregularly.

Is it possible to become pregnant while going through menopause?

A woman going through menopause can become pregnant. If a woman has not menstruated for at least a year following menopause, a pregnancy is highly unlikely.

After menopause, why do some women take hormones, and what hormones do they take?

To eliminate or reduce the number and intensity of hot flashes for a woman at the age of menopause, a doctor may prescribe artificial hormones — estrogen and progesterone pills — so that hormone levels are equalized and then remain nearly constant.

CHAPTER 7

MENSTRUATION

What is menstruation and why does it occur?

Menstruation is the monthly shedding of the uterus lining, which is made of blood and tissue. It begins at puberty, when a female starts producing enough special hormones (chemical messengers carried in the bloodstream) to cause the start of this blood flow. (See also The Female Body section of Chapter 3.)

In a normal female, the process of releasing an egg, called ovulation, begins when the inner lining of the uterus (the womb) prepares itself for a possible pregnancy by building up blood and tissue. This buildup could nourish a fertilized egg. If fertilization does not occur, there is no need for this enriched lining, so it automatically leaves the body, along with the unfertilized egg, in the form of menstrual blood flow.

Various hormones produced by the body trigger the menstrual flow, which usually begins about two weeks after ovulation. Some young females, before they even begin to ovulate, produce enough hormones — particularly the one called estrogen — to build up the lining of the uterus and cause menstrual bleeding.

A hormone called progesterone, which is produced when fertilization does not occur, is needed to stop bleeding. Young females who have not started to ovulate do not produce much progesterone, so their first few menstrual periods may last longer and be heavier than normal. For example, a period may last ten days rather than four to six, and sanitary napkins or tampons may need to be changed often. If the flow is extremely heavy and goes on longer than ten days, a young woman should go to a doctor or nurse practitioner.

Where did menstruation get its name?

The word "menstruation" comes from *mensis,* a Latin term meaning "month." The English word "menses" means "menstrual periods."

Is there a difference between a menstrual period and a menstrual cycle?

Yes. The *period* refers to the time when a female is menstruating. The menstrual *cycle,* which is usually twenty-eight to thirty days long, is the complete chain of events, from the beginning of one flow to the beginning of the next. Day 1 of the menstrual cycle would be the first day of the period. Day 5 or 6 would be the end of the period. The nonbleeding portion of the cycle would run from Day 6 to Day 28 or Day 30, with Day 28 or 30 being the final day of the cycle, just before the next bleeding.

How often does menstruation occur?

A menstrual cycle can occur approximately every twenty-six to thirty days. There are some females who will be irregular: they may have a thirty-day cycle for a while and then maybe a forty-day cycle, then perhaps skip a month. It is impossible to say that once the menstrual cycle is under way an individual is going to be absolutely regular. We can say that if the mother or sister has regular periods, another female in the family is likely to have a regular cycle. It is the exceptional woman who is absolutely regular every month — someone who could predict, for example, that she will begin her period at 4 P.M. every fourth Tuesday. That can happen, but it is most unusual.

The first few periods can be irregular. As has been said, they may last a little longer and the flow may be a little heavier. Try thinking of the menstrual cycle as a clock that needs to be set just right for a particular person's body. It might take a year or two to set this "menstrual clock" on its schedule. Imagine a clock you might have at home: although it never quite keeps the "right" time — maybe it is a little slow, a little fast, a little behind or ahead — it is still "normal" once you get used to it.

How long does a normal period last?

It lasts four to six days; five days is considered an average menstrual period. Women who take birth-control pills may have periods with light flow that last fewer than five days. A normal period, however, should not last more than seven days.

Why do some people call the menstrual period "the curse"?

The term "curse" probably came from the fact that having a menstrual period can be inconvenient. There are some people who say that this term is derived from the biblical belief that a menstrual period was "forced" upon Eve as a part of her punishment for sin. There are many other slang and vulgar expressions for menstruating, including "having my friend" and "being on the rag." Most young women simply call it their "period."

At what age does menstruation usually begin?

Typically, females get their periods between the ages of twelve and a half and thirteen, but there always are some who begin as early as ten, a few even earlier. On the other hand, some females may not begin to menstruate until age fifteen or sixteen. It all depends on the production and release of hormones. If bleeding occurs before a girl is ten, her mother should take her to see a doctor to make sure that such an early start is part of normal development.

Likewise, a female who is fifteen and has not had a period may want to check with her doctor. Menstruation can be delayed for a number of reasons: strenuous physical activity, low body weight, a medical problem, or heredity.

Is it possible never to start having periods?

Females who never have menstrual periods almost always are born with a genetic disorder, an abnormality or disease that is the result of a family problem or a defect in their genes. An endocrinologist (a physician specializing in problems involving the hormone systems) or a geneticist (a scientist specializing in problems of the basic units of heredity, the chromosomes and genes) usually can find why a female has never had a menstrual period.

What are physical signs that the first period is about to start?

It can be difficult to identify physical signs indicating when the first period is near. Many females say that before their periods they have some lower abdominal pain or some breast tenderness. Others say they have a feeling that something is going to happen. Before puberty all females will have some normal vaginal mucus discharge, but it is difficult to say if there is more discharge just before the first period.

Do body weight and fat have anything to do with beginning to menstruate?

Since a certain minimum weight is necessary to prepare the body for a normal pregnancy, the first requirement is a healthy female. A female's nutrition may not be adequate if she is low in weight in relation to her height. You might say that the body protects itself by not allowing an underweight female to menstruate. Even if other signs indicate that puberty has begun, the beginning of menstruation may be delayed.

Females with eating disorders, such as anorexia nervosa (inability or unwillingness to eat), or female athletes who have a limited amount of fat tissue may not begin their menstrual periods at the normal age. For some of these females, their periods may be interrupted until they regain normal weight or body fat.

What should a young woman do when she has her first period?

The first thing she should do is talk about it with her mother or with another close female relative or friend, or both. Even better, she should talk about it before the first period begins. It always helps to be prepared, so before a young woman's first menstrual period, her mother should take time to talk with her about menstruation. It is important, too, ahead of time, for her family doctor, pediatrician, or nurse practitioner to discuss menstruation with her and give her helpful information to read. Similar information about health issues almost always is available in the library, from the school nurse, and from manufacturers of sanitary products.

Is is normal to be afraid of the first menstrual period?

Of course; it is normal to be concerned about anything that is unfamiliar or new. That's why being well informed can make such a difference. When a young woman knows what to expect, she usually feels more confident and less anxious or worried than someone who has not had chances for discussion and reading or has not taken a sex education class.

Should a sanitary pad or a tampon be used for the first few menstrual periods?

Most young women would probably prefer using a sanitary pad — again, keeping in mind that the first period may be a little heavier than usual because it often occurs without ovulation, and only a small amount of progesterone, the hormone that stops the flow, is produced. If a young woman prefers tampons, that's fine — there is no reason to avoid them. This is a decision that each female makes for herself.

Sanitary pads, sometimes called sanitary napkins, are rectangular cotton pads that come in various sizes and thicknesses; they are often lined on a single side or in the middle with a plastic film. Some pads are held in place by an elastic belt, called a sanitary belt, and others by an adhesive strip that sticks to the underpants. They are worn inside the underpants to soak up the menstrual flow.

A tampon is a very slim, two- to three-inch-long tube of compressed soft cotton, which is inserted into the vagina. The tampon goes in by using an applicator or by pushing it in place with the fingers. As the tampon soaks up the menstrual flow, it expands like a sponge. The tampon can be removed by gently pulling an attached string that extends a few inches out of the vagina. Sometimes, if a young woman has an extra heavy flow, she may want to wear a pad and a tampon.

After using pads for the first several periods, a young woman may decide to switch to tampons for comfort and convenience. Tampons come in various absorbencies. To minimize the possibility of infection, they should be left in place no longer than six to eight hours. Toxic shock syndrome is a serious infection that can result if a tampon is left in the vagina for a prolonged period of time. However, toxic shock syndrome rarely occurs anymore because the directions about safe use of tampons are well known (see the notice accompanying all tampon boxes) and hazardous materials are no longer used in making them.

How old should a female be before she begins using tampons?

That depends upon when a female begins her menstrual cycle, which may be as early as ten or eleven years of age or as late as fourteen or fifteen. Many females prefer to use sanitary napkins when they first begin to menstruate, but tampons can be used just as well from the start.

Can virgins use tampons?

In most cases, virgins can — and do — use tampons without tearing the hymen.

Which is safer, more hygienic, and more effective — a tampon or a sanitary napkin?

Tampons and sanitary napkins are both safe, hygienic, and effective if properly used. Deciding which to use is almost always a matter of personal preference and convenience. Quite often if menstrual flow is heavy, a sanitary napkin or a combination of a napkin and a tampon can be worn. As long as tampons are used according to the instructions provided in the package insert — especially changing them as frequently as indicated — there is little, if any, danger of infection.

How often should a woman change her sanitary napkin?

That depends upon how heavy or light the menstrual flow happens to be. With a heavy flow, a young woman would want to change napkins every hour or two. When the flow decreases, napkins can be changed every six to eight hours. Since sanitary napkins are worn outside the body, there is little risk of infection.

How often should tampons be changed?

Tampons should be changed every four to six hours. If tampons are improperly used they can cause problems. Infections in the vagina have a tendency to occur if tampons are not changed regularly.

Do deodorant tampons provide extra cleanliness?

Deodorant tampons function in the same way as other tampons. The addition of deodorant is not harmful and makes no difference as far as hygiene is concerned.

Can a tampon move so high into the body that the string disappears?

It is possible for a tampon to move so high into the vagina that the string used for removal is no longer visible. If this happens, it often is possible for the young woman to reach into the vagina with her finger and retrieve the tampon, perhaps using her pelvic muscles to help push it out. If the young woman cannot reach the tampon, she should see a doctor or nurse, who can carefully remove it.

Why is menstrual flow sometimes brown instead of red?

The flow may range in color from dark red to brown because blood tends to change color after a certain length of time — it doesn't stay bright red. This has to do with a chemical change in the hemoglobin, the oxygen-carrying part of the blood. A heavy menstrual flow may be dark red, but if it is bright red and continues to be bright red, a doctor should be consulted.

Is it normal to have blood clots in the flow?

Let's say that it's not *abnormal* to have clots in the flow. Normal human blood has a tendency to clot because of special chemicals in the blood that are necessary for healing. When a small cut bleeds, the bleeding soon slows, then stops, and the wound closes because of the clotting action. Menstrual flow is similar: some of this blood will become organized into blood clots, and the clots may be numerous and thick. If a female ever notices that the clots are more numerous and different from any she has seen before, she should check with a doctor.

Occasionally, particular clots may be the result of a miscarriage (the spontaneous termination of a pregnancy). Some women who have had a particularly heavy period may, in fact, have gone through a miscarriage without ever being aware that they were pregnant.

What determines the amount of menstrual flow each month?

The amount depends on many things, including the effects of hormones, whether or not ovulation has occurred, and heredity. A female can judge whether her flow is light, moderate, or heavy by the number of sanitary pads or tampons she uses in a day. A light period would require no more than two pads a day, a medium period would be three, a heavy period five or more. It's impossible to estimate the "average" amount with any accuracy.

Why is there sometimes an odor during menstruation?

Body odor need not be a problem during menstruation, especially when normal hygiene — bathing and showering — is followed. If there is a body odor, it could be caused by neglecting hygiene. The menstrual flow itself has no odor unless a sanitary pad is left in place too long or underwear becomes stained. A vaginal yeast infection or some other type of vaginal problem could have odor associated with it. If the odor is quite noticeable, or if it persists after menstruation, a vaginal infection may be present, and a doctor should be consulted.

Why do breasts become tender just before and during a menstrual period?

Breasts can be tender as a result of the rise in the amount of estrogen. Breast tenderness should disappear when the period is over.

Can having her period make a female feel physically ill?

Certainly some individuals may feel bloated or crampy during their menstrual periods, but most females should not feel so sick that normal activities must be limited. Young women who regularly feel ill during their periods should see a doctor, who can explain the problem, provide emotional support, and perhaps prescribe medication. In most cases, the problem can be relieved. A careful physical exam and evaluation usually can be done to help alleviate or cure any problem related to menstruation.

What causes menstrual cramps?

Cramps are caused by monthly physical changes in the body related to the menstrual cycle. The muscular walls of the uterus gently contract to help remove the lining. Menstrual cramps usually occur at the onset of the menstrual flow. Cramps may affect a woman at any age. Some females, unfortunately, have severe cramps, and they should seek a doctor's help and receive pain-relieving medication.

Why do cramps occur only at the beginning of a period?

Cramps sometimes occur when the body releases the hormone progesterone — at the start of a period. As the amount of progesterone activity decreases toward the end of the period, cramps fade and disappear.

Is it normal *not* to have cramps?

Of course; cramps do not automatically come with a female's menstrual period. Some young women never have cramps, while others have them either regularly or from time to time.

How should a female treat cramps?

For moderate to mild cramps, the common nonprescription pain-relievers, such as aspirin, acetaminophen, and ibuprofen, usually are effective. If a particular pain-reliever does not help a young woman after two or more periods with cramps, she should check with a doctor or nurse practitioner.

Do periods really cause females to become more emotional?

The monthly rise in hormones may be connected with physical problems, such as cramps, a bloated stomach, or pimples, and can make some females feel irritable, short-tempered, a little grumpy, or even like they want to cry. Some females say they feel "out of control" just before or during their periods.

What effect does stress have on the menstrual period?

Stress, caused by mental or physical strain or tension, often makes a difficult or painful situation worse. For instance, some teens who tend to get menstrual cramps may find that the cramps become more bothersome if there is a test coming up, if they have an argument with a sibling or friend, or if they are in some other potentially stressful situation.

What is premenstrual syndrome?

Premenstrual syndrome (PMS) is the regular occurrence of certain problems before menstruation or in the early days of a female's period. These problems may include abdominal bloating, backache, weight gain, breast tenderness, acne, asthma, constipation, cravings for sweet and salty foods, headache, irritability, fatigue, tension, anxiety, lethargy, and depression. Some doctors believe that PMS affects half of all females at some time during their reproductive years. About 5 percent of those females who experience PMS may be forced to reduce their normal activities because they are so severely affected. Although the exact cause of PMS remains unknown, a number of theories are under investigation. PMS may be related to the monthly rise in hormone level, to low blood sugar, to a vitamin deficiency, to a temporary change in the delicate biochemicals in the brain affecting mood, to a combination of these factors, or to none of them.

Is it a sign that something is wrong if a period is early or late?

If a menstrual period is a day or two early or late, there is no cause for concern. For the young woman who has had recent sexual relations, a delay might be a sign of pregnancy. If a female skips more than two periods in a row or suspects she is pregnant, she should consult a doctor. Sometimes simply worrying about the possibility of pregnancy can delay a period. On the other hand, if a young woman's period is early, and flow continues for a long time — perhaps ten or twelve days — she should see a doctor.

What can cause a woman to miss a period?

A variety of situations or problems may interfere with a normal menstrual cycle, and, depending upon how quickly the problem is resolved, a woman's period usually returns. Missing one period most likely signifies nothing, unless, of course, a woman has been sexually active and might be pregnant. If a female who has had regular periods, and has not been sexually active, misses her period for more than three months, she should see a doctor.

Will a period return if it has stopped for a long time?

A menstrual period can be interrupted for many months — even years — because of an endocrine problem, chronic illness, intensive medical treatment (such as chemotherapy or radiation therapy), an eating disorder, or intensive athletic training. Regular periods may resume after the problem is resolved.

If periods have not occurred for more than a year, and a young woman has had a careful medical exam to rule out physical problems that could cause the lack of periods, a doctor might consider hormone treatment.

Can something be taken to delay menstruation?

No. For a specific illness, a doctor might prescribe a certain medicine that could have the side effect of interfering with the menstrual period. That type of delay does not often happen to a teenager.

Can other people tell when a woman is having her period?

Usually not — with some exceptions. If a female has a relative or friend who knows her very well — mother, sister, girlfriend, boyfriend, aunt — and that person notices that her personality or mood is a little different at a certain time each month, then this could be a sign of menstruation. So-called telltale signs vary: perhaps a female feels cranky, upset, or has a few extra pimples. It is nearly impossible for a casual acquaintance or a stranger to tell whether a female is having her period just from her physical appearance.

Is bathing or showering safe — in either cold or hot water — during a period?

Certainly it's safe to take any kind of shower or bath: hot, cold, or in between. Some people may claim that if you take a cold bath it will stop your period, or that if you take a hot bath your period will last longer. For the most part, these claims are nonsense.

Are there some activities that a young woman should avoid while she is having her period?

During the menstrual period, females can participate in all activities, including sports, unless, of course, there is great discomfort.

Is it OK to exercise during menstruation?

By all means! There is no reason not to exercise. It will not affect a menstrual period, and, for most females, having a menstrual period should not affect athletic performance. Even more important, exercise can make a person feel better. Physical activity is good for the body.

Can a young woman have intercourse during her period?

There is no health reason that would prohibit intercourse during a menstrual period. Whether to have intercourse is more a matter of aesthetics — how it looks and feels. A female might feel that at certain times intercourse would not be satisfying or pleasing. However, if the flow is light and the male and female are both agreeable, intercourse during a period is possible.

Can a woman leave a tampon in while having intercourse?

It is physically possible to leave a tampon in place during intercourse, but it certainly is not recommended. Tampons left in the vagina during intercourse, accidentally or intentionally, can cause infection and discharge, particularly if the partner is infected with a sexually transmitted disease.

Does intercourse cause the flow to stop?

Having intercourse does not stop menstrual bleeding.

CHAPTER 8

HYGIENE, HEALTH, AND MEDICINE

Why do adolescents get acne?

Acne is an increased response of the body's sweat and oil glands to the heightened level of sex hormone, specifically testosterone, the male hormone. Remember that females have a small amount of male hormone in their bodies, and this small amount may be enough to cause the outbreak of acne. Females who experience severe acne may have a history of acne in their families, so that it can be assumed that the cause is hereditary.

Does acne have anything to do with sexual activity?

No.

Is acne contagious?

No.

Is cotton underwear better than other kinds for men and women?

Cotton underwear, because it is porous and "breathes," is often recommended for males and females who have skin irritations or infections. Cotton may also be the best choice for people who are active and perspire a great deal. However, for people with normal skin, most types of comfortably fitting underwear are satisfactory as long as they are clean.

Are tight jeans, leotards, tights, or panty hose a health hazard?

Tight jeans, especially if worn without underwear, can be irritating and lead to infection. Chafing and possible reduction of blood supply can lead to fungus infections for males and females and to urinary tract and vaginal infections for females. Leotards and tights are not a hazard as long as they are clean. Panty hose should not pose a problem as long as they are clean and are designed to "breathe," especially in the area of the crotch. Most styles of panty hose come with a cotton insert for that purpose.

What is oral herpes?

Oral herpes (HER-peez) is cold sores or fever blisters that are caused by a virus known as herpes simplex. The virus causes painful blisters around the mouth and nose and occasionally inside the mouth. Oral herpes is often associated with respiratory infection or fever. Some people can have oral herpes flare up as a result of sun and wind exposure. The condition can, and usually does, recur among susceptible people.

Can oral herpes be spread by kissing an infected person?

Yes. In fact, this is a common means of contracting oral herpes.

Can oral herpes be transmitted by using an infected person's toothbrush?

Yes. The spread of infectious disease through sharing of toothbrushes is fairly common. It is a good idea to dispose of your toothbrush after recovering from any infectious disease. All toothbrushes should be replaced every three or four months, and for the sake of good hygiene, toothbrushes should not be shared.

What causes rashes and sores that sometimes appear on the body?

Rashes and sores can be caused by a variety of different things, such as allergies, stress, viruses, and fungus. Unexplained rashes or sores that appear anywhere on the body and do not clear up quickly need to be evaluated and treated by a physician.

HYGIENE AND HEALTH FOR FEMALES

Why do some females shave their underarms, legs, or pubic hair?

Shaving underarms and legs is a matter of personal preference. Excess pubic hair may be shaved for cosmetic purposes (that is, for the sake of appearance), especially in the summer if bikini bathing suits are to be worn. There is no particular health advantage or disadvantage in a female's shaving various types of body hair.

What are some methods of hair removal?

Careful shaving of underarm hair and hair on the legs is safe, even though there is no health necessity for doing so. Underarm and leg shaving is done for cosmetic and fashion reasons. To avoid irritation or rash, deodorant or antiperspirant should not be used immediately after shaving under the arms. Hair removal creams, called depilatories (dee-PILL-a-tories), also are sometimes used to remove hair. There are some problems with this method, since skin irritation, including reddening of the skin, can occur. Shaving or using depilatories for facial hair is not a good idea for females because coarsening and thickening of the new growth often occurs. Careful tweezing of a few individual hairs usually does not cause any problems. Special facial bleaches can be used to lighten dark facial hair.

Is it safe for a female to use wax to remove hair?

Waxing is a process in which special heated wax is applied to an area of the body. When the wax is removed, the hairs come out with it. Waxing usually causes no problems, except for some minor skin irritation, if it is done carefully by a well-trained person. Some people, however, say that waxing can be a bit painful when the hairs are pulled out.

Should facial hair on females ever be removed permanently?

Unwanted hair, regardless of location, should be evaluated by a dermatologist before a decision is made about possible permanent removal. Electrolysis (elec-TROL-a-sis) removes hair permanently by destroying the hair root with a fine electric needle. Permanent hair removal through electrolysis, which can be somewhat painful, should be done only by an experienced professional because of the risk of infection and the likelihood that scars will form. Battery-operated hair removal machines designed for home use are not recommended.

What are douches?

A douche (DOOSH) is any one of a number of different kinds of fluids that are used to flush out the vagina.

What are douches used for?

A female may use a douche occasionally to remove a substance from the vagina which she considers uncomfortable or undesirable, such as some type of discharge. Douches are sometimes mistakenly used as a contraceptive, but they are not effective at all in preventing pregnancy.

Are douches safe?

A douche may be safe as long as it contains no chemicals that could irritate the vagina. The use of a douche for an adolescent, however, is not recommended unless specifically prescribed by a doctor.

Should women use feminine hygiene sprays?

Feminine hygiene sprays are not effective, necessary, or appropriate for young women. If a female uses a spray for the single purpose of improving her overall feeling of cleanliness or freshness, taking a shower or using a simple powder would be more effective, safer, and less expensive. If a female has a vaginal discharge that she finds unpleasant or annoying, a doctor should be consulted to diagnose the condition causing the odor.

What would cause a female to have bleeding while urinating?

Bleeding while urinating means that there is a tear or inflammation in the lining of the bladder or urinary tract. Such bleeding could be caused by injury or infection. It is important to find out whether the bleeding accompanies urination or if it originates somewhere in the vagina. For example, there may be some blood in the urine during the menstrual period.

What does it mean if a female has some spotting between periods?

Spotting, or bleeding from the vagina between periods, could mean many things. For example, it is not unusual for a female who has recently begun taking birth-control pills to notice some spotting. But if spotting occurs frequently or is excessive, it is important for a female to consult a physician.

Is it possible for a female to urinate while she is having sex?

This occurs only if there is something wrong with the urinary system. During intercourse physical strain may trigger urination. If a female has some sort of urinary problem, she should urinate before having intercourse.

Is a white discharge normal for females?

It is normal to have a certain amount of discharge through-out the menstrual cycle. This is natural lubricating fluid, composed of a clear mucous substance and perhaps some cells from the lining of the vagina. The exact color of the discharge is not as important as whether there is an unusually large volume and whether it has a strong odor. If the discharge seems unusual a female should consult a physician.

What is an unusual amount of discharge, and what might it indicate?

A large volume (more than perhaps a tablespoonful, which might require the use of a sanitary pad to absorb it) and a strong odor could indicate the presence of infection. If the female has been sexually active, there is a possibility that an unusual dis-charge could be a sign of a sexually transmitted disease.

What is a gynecologic exam?

A gynecologic (guy-na-co-LOJ-ic) exam is a medical exam-ination of a female's reproductive system. During childhood, in the course of regular physical exams, a doctor or nurse practitioner should regularly check a girl's genital organs to make sure that growth and development are on schedule. A doctor or nurse practitioner can quickly and painlessly check the vagina and in-ternal genital organs throughout childhood as well as explain and discuss the structure of the reproductive system with the help of an anatomical model.

The first routine gynecologic exam usually is performed at about the age of seventeen or eighteen, the final year in high school, or earlier if the female is sexually active or has had a problem such as vaginal discharge, unusual vaginal bleeding, irregular or absent periods, or abdominal pain. A doctor or nurse practitioner performs the examination. The whole process often is simply called a pelvic exam or vaginal exam.

After other phases of the customary physical exam are completed, including checking the breasts for lumps, the female is asked to lie on her back on an examining table. The young woman places her feet in metal stirrups at the left and right corners of the table and is asked by the doctor or nurse to keep her knees apart. The doctor or nurse will slowly, gently insert a gloved, lubricated finger in the outside of the vagina to check the external genital organs. Then with a special examining instrument called a speculum (SPECK-you-lum), the cervix can be viewed. The speculum, made of plastic or metal, separates the walls of the vagina just enough so that the internal reproductive organs are easy to see. If the hymen is present and has not been broken, the doctor or nurse will not try to go any further but will be satisfied with what is visible.

The doctor or nurse then gently inserts one or two gloved, lubricated fingers into the vagina and with the other hand presses down on the abdomen above the pelvis to feel the size and position of the uterus, the fallopian tubes, and the ovaries, and to check for swelling, tenderness, or abnormal growths. (This is called a two-hand exam.) Sometimes, the examiner places one finger in the rectum and another in the vagina while pressing down with the other hand. This maneuver checks the condition of the tissue wall separating the vagina and rectum. Finally, the doctor or nurse may perform a rectal exam, which involves inserting one gloved, lubricated finger and feeling inside the anus and rectum for the presence of lumps, swelling, or obstruction.

During all internal exams, young women can concentrate on reducing physical tension and discomfort by taking a series of long, slow, deep breaths. Emotional tension often can be eased by communication. It is helpful to keep talking with the doctor or nurse practitioner during the examination and to ask questions or share concerns. The doctor or nurse practitioner should explain everything that takes place during an examination.

What is a Pap smear?

While the doctor or nurse practitioner views the cervix through the speculum, a Pap smear, a procedure to collect some cells lining the cervix, is taken. (The test is named for Dr. G. N. Papanicolaou, who perfected this examination.) The doctor or nurse practitioner uses a long cotton-tipped swab or wooden applicator to scrape some cells gently from the surface tissue of the cervix. These cells are transferred to a microscope slide that is sent to a laboratory for analysis. (If any abnormal or unusual cells are identified, the doctor or nurse notifies the individual as soon as the report is received from the lab.) A Pap smear is taken during the gynecologic exam, but usually not more often than once every twelve to twenty-four months for a teenager, unless particular problems have to be checked.

In addition to the Pap smear, cultures of the vagina and cervix may be taken to check for the presence of sexually transmitted diseases (also called venereal diseases) in sexually active young women. This simply involves touching a cotton swab to the lining of the vagina and cervix and sending the samples to a lab for analysis. A doctor may also want to take a small amount of fluid from the vagina to secure cell samples.

Does the doctor break the hymen during the exam?

No, there is usually no need to do so. If the hymen is tight or has a very small opening, the doctor or nurse practitioner can show the young woman how to dilate (enlarge) it.

How should a female examine her breasts?

The breasts can be examined anytime a female takes a bath or shower. It is a good idea to examine the breasts carefully once every three to six months. It is effective to always examine them at the same stage in the menstrual cycle — the first week after the menstrual period is often the best time because breasts tend to be smallest and least sensitive to pressure at this time. Breasts change and may feel different at various times during the menstrual cycle. Just before a woman's period, for example, her breasts may become tender and slightly enlarged.

A woman can examine her breasts by feeling all parts of them with the fingertips, using circular motions. This should be done in the shower, standing up, and then lying down. Anytime what appears to be a lump is detected, a doctor should be consulted. Most lumps turn out to be harmless, but each one should be evaluated by a doctor. Some females tend to have more breast lumps than others, and they need to have these lumps checked regularly. (See Figure 3.)

Is a discharge from nipples normal?

Except during pregnancy or while breast feeding, a discharge from nipples is not normal or common, especially if it persists. The cause of most nipple discharges is production of hormones — usually prolactin, which is formed in the pituitary gland in the brain. Prolactin production is a normal part of pregnancy, making it possible for a woman to nurse an infant. But for a female who is not pregnant, prolactin production and breast discharge are abnormal and should be checked by a doctor.

What can be done to make the breasts larger?

Some young females may not develop what they consider to be desirable breast size — usually they want larger breasts than they currently have — but their breasts *are* totally normal. They look fine and function normally. Teenagers should not purchase any of the breast creams or exotic devices, or believe in strange exercises or diets that promise a dramatic increase in breast size. To a healthy female who has perfectly normal breasts, these are only empty promises.

Breasts stop developing when puberty ends — that means when growth of the body and skeleton is completed. However, certain conditions can affect breast size, such as being overweight or pregnant. Exercise does not significantly influence breast size, although toning and developing the pectoral muscles can bring about a small increase. If a female takes birth-control pills, her breasts may increase slightly in size.

Can very large breasts be reduced in size?

Although so-called small breasts trouble many females, there also are some who have breasts that they think are too large. Large-breasted teenagers may be embarrassed, and they may, for example, feel uncomfortable being seen in a bathing suit for fear of what others may say or think. Although surgery can reduce breast size, this option is usually not recommended for very young women.

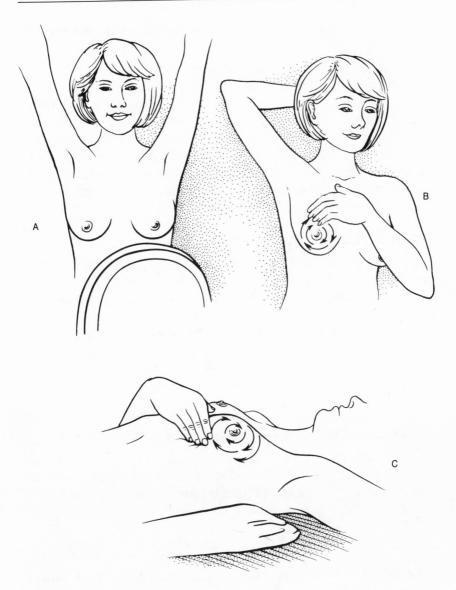

FIGURE 3. Breast Self-examination.

A. By raising the arms and looking at her breasts in a mirror, a woman can note even slight changes, such as dimples or pulling of the nipple.

B. A circular, massaging motion should be used while standing, preferably in the shower using soap and water.

C. A woman should use a circular, massaging motion with one hand over each breast.

Is there any danger from going braless even after the breasts are developed?

No specific physical danger is associated with going braless. Sometimes, going braless can be uncomfortable, especially for large-breasted females. The young female who has large breasts and does not wear a bra might speed the sagging of her breasts by the continued pulling of gravity. Wearing a bra can probably help the larger-breasted young female remain firmer longer. Females with breasts of average size can maintain their breast profile by maintaining good health, sound nutrition, and normal weight, and by getting adequate exercise.

What is DES and what effect does it have?

Diethylstilbestrol, usually called DES, is a synthetic female hormone. About thirty years ago, DES was given to women who had had spontaneous abortions or complicated pregnancies to prevent further difficulties, especially miscarriages. Years later, the children of these women, especially their daughters, began to have severe problems, especially with cancer of the lining of vagina and cervix. Because of the link between DES and these problems, DES has not been prescribed since the early 1960s, so it is not a problem for teenagers today.

What would cause internal pain during intercourse?

A woman may feel some internal pain the first time she has intercourse. This may be caused when the penis stretches or tears an intact hymen. If internal pain is routinely experienced during intercourse, a doctor should be consulted.

HYGIENE AND HEALTH FOR MALES

Should a male wear an athletic supporter (jockstrap) while participating in sports?

Athletic supporters protect the genital organs by holding the penis and scrotum snugly in place. This eases the strain on the scrotum and testicles caused by the twisting, turning, and bouncing that are part of many sports. Playing contact sports such as football and wrestling often makes it necessary for an athlete to wear a plastic cup for extra protection.

What does a cup do?

A cup, usually made from plastic or metal, provides the penis and scrotum with greater protection from direct physical blows or pounding in contact sports such as boxing, wrestling, judo, and football.

What is jock itch, and is it contagious?

Wearing a tight jockstrap or tight briefs can irritate the skin. Sometimes this irritation is followed by a fungal infection, which causes intense itching, known as jock itch. Particularly sensitive areas include the inner thighs and the genital area. This fungal infection can be treated with medicine that is applied as an ointment, a powder, or a spray. Jock itch is contagious and can be transmitted if underwear or jockstraps worn by someone with jock itch are not first laundered thoroughly in detergent and hot water before being worn by someone else.

Can a male get a disease from not washing his penis regularly?

Proper general hygiene, which includes regularly washing the penis, is always important. This is especially important for males who are uncircumcised. Ordinarily, however, a male would not acquire a specific disease as a result of not washing his penis.

What is circumcision?

Circumcision is the surgical removal of the foreskin, which naturally covers the head (glans) of the penis. If parents choose to have their son circumcised, it can be done before the baby leaves the hospital or in a clinic following birth — that is, within the first two or three days of life — or it may be performed within the first eight to ten days of life. Circumcision may be performed by an obstetrician (a doctor who delivers babies), by a surgeon, or by an individual specially trained to perform circumcision as part of a religious ritual.

Why do boys get circumcised?

Circumcision is performed because the doctor or parents feel that it is beneficial for health, religious, or cultural reasons. There is little medical basis for choosing circumcision. Except in a very small number of instances, males have little trouble keeping the head (glans) of the penis clean by gently retracting the foreskin and washing underneath. Members of the Jewish and Moslem religions choose to have their males circumcised as part of a religious ritual.

Are circumcised males cleaner than uncircumcised males?

With proper care, uncircumcised males of all ages can be as clean as those who are circumcised.

Are more boys circumcised or uncircumcised?

There currently are more circumcised than uncircumcised boys in the United States. For decades circumcision was performed routinely on nearly all males born in U.S. hospitals, but there is now a trend away from that practice. Many physicians view circumcision as an unnecessary, painful health risk, no matter how minor. The American Academy of Pediatrics has stated that "there is no medical indication for routine circumcision of the newborn." Despite this, it is estimated that the majority of newborn boys in the United States, about 60 percent, continue to be circumcised. So it seems that circumcised boys will continue to outnumber uncircumcised boys for at least another decade or so.

Does circumcision affect sexual performance or pleasure?

Folklore and mythology suggest that circumcised males experience greater sexual pleasure because of a higher degree of sensitivity in the head of the penis. There is no reliable evidence to support claims that circumcision improves or detracts from sexual pleasure.

What is an undescended testicle?

Sometimes boys are born with a testicle that is not in the scrotum where it belongs. While a male is developing in the womb, his testicles move from the abdomen, where they develop, to the scrotum. At birth, both testicles should be in the scrotum, but one boy in every two hundred has a testicle that is not. An undescended testicle usually can be moved into the scrotum with surgery. If the operation takes place before the boy is six years old, the chances are good that the testicle will be healthy and produce sperm.

What would cause a thirteen-year-old male's breasts to hurt?

Boys between twelve and fifteen years of age may notice some swelling and tenderness under the nipple on one or both sides, and they may be concerned that they are developing breasts. This development is called gynecomastia (guy-na-co-MAS-ti-a), meaning excessive breast development in the male. This happens to 40 to 60 percent of all growing boys during early puberty. The small amount of estrogen that a developing male possesses can cause minor breast development. Gynecomastia disappears without treatment.

If tenderness or pain occurs and there has been no injury, it makes sense to see a doctor if the pain does not go away within four to six weeks. A doctor should also be consulted if slight breast swelling does not go away after a year or two. Perhaps 1 to 2 percent of boys with gynecomastia might require plastic surgery to remove unwanted breast tissue. For boys who are overweight, what may appear to be breast tissue is really fat, and surgery is not recommended in these cases.

If a male doesn't ejaculate when he masturbates or when he has an erection, can he get clogged up?

No. This question probably stems from a worry that if a male's seminal fluid does not find an outlet, he will not be able to urinate or ejaculate normally. That simply does not happen. As most males discover, delaying or postponing ejaculation is not easy to do. In fact, during masturbation nearly all men find it difficult to stop at the point when ejaculation is about to occur because ejaculation takes place involuntarily. But if masturbation does not lead to ejaculation, for whatever reason, the seminal fluid is retained in the seminal vesicles or absorbed, and clogging or congestion is not a problem.

What should a male do if he experiences pain when he ejaculates?

Painful ejaculation is a problem that needs to be evaluated by a physician.

What is impotence?

Impotence (im-puh-tense) is the inability to achieve and maintain an erection for sexual intercourse.

What causes impotence?

Impotence can be temporary, caused, for example, by use of alcohol or drugs, fatigue, or emotional problems. Reactions to medical treatments or medicines also can cause temporary impotence. An injury or a physical defect may cause permanent impotence. In any case, a doctor should be consulted for an evaluation and perhaps for referral to an experienced counselor.

Is impotence related to sterility?

Impotence is not related to sterility. Males who are sterile usually are able to achieve and maintain an erection and engage in sexual intercourse, but they do not produce sperm. Those who are impotent cannot achieve and maintain an erection but usually do not have a fertility problem.

What percentage of the male population is impotent?

There are statistics estimating what percentage of the adult male population is impotent, but it always is difficult to know how accurate the figures are. It is safe to say that impotence is unusual among young males.

Can impotence be treated? If so, how?

Impotence often can be treated successfully with the right approach and under the right conditions. First, discussions with a counselor can help sort out emotional problems or conflicts. Then, some sessions with a qualified sex therapist might be helpful. Sex therapists have developed a number of techniques, including suggestions about physical approach, visualization, and "sensate focus" (concentrating on ways of becoming physically and emotionally aroused), which can enable males who have no physical problem to achieve and maintain an erection.

CHAPTER 9

SEXUAL ACTIVITIES

What are sexual activities, and why are they so important?

Sexual activities are physical or mental actions that are stimulating, arousing, and physically exciting. These actions serve as an important way for someone to express feelings and attraction for another person. Many people engage in sexual activities, either alone or with another person, simply because they are pleasurable. In addition, certain sexual activities, specifically sexual intercourse, are necessary for reproduction. (See Chapter 2, "Thoughts, Feelings, and Concerns of Teenagers," and Chapter 4, "What Is Sexuality?")

What is masturbation?

Masturbation is stimulating the genital (sex) organs, usually with the hand, without engaging in sexual intercourse. For the male, masturbation is stimulating the penis by stroking or rubbing it. For the female, masturbation usually includes fondling and stroking the genital area, especially the clitoris and vagina. Masturbation is usually considered to be a self-stimulating act, but sometimes one partner will stimulate the other partner's genitals, possibly resulting in orgasm.

Masturbation for males has many slang names, which are considered vulgar, such as "beat off," "beat your meat," "jerk off," "jack off," "flub the dub," and "whack off." Masturbation for males and females sometimes may be called "playing with yourself."

What does masturbation feel like, and does it feel different from sex with a partner?

Masturbation provides a pleasurable feeling; otherwise, people would not engage in it. Physically, an orgasm from masturbation feels much like an orgasm from sexual intercourse, but the emotional impact is different. Instead of experiencing pleasure or relief alone — as usually happens in masturbation — sex with a partner involves *mutual* pleasure.

Is it "normal" to masturbate?

Masturbation is a normal part of self-discovery, and, although not essential to the physical process of human sexual development, it is a common activity among both males and females. It may have positive psychological value in that it provides a way of relieving sexual tension and releasing sexual energy.

Are there any physical side effects to masturbation — for example, blindness, hair growth, or harm to the genitals?

There are no so-called physical side effects to masturbation. Even the choice of the term "side effects" indicates a moralistic, critical attitude that masturbation must be an abnormality. It is not unusual during adolescence for both males and females to feel guilty or ashamed following masturbation. This guilt usually stems from teenagers believing that their parents or other adults would disapprove of the action or because of the social stigma attached to masturbation.

In fact, it is common for a teenager who feels guilty to worry that some minor physical defect, real or imagined, is caused by genital self-stimulation. It seems likely that these myths will persist, especially among young males and females. For example, it is often rumored — mistakenly — that people who masturbate will go blind or crazy, grow hair on the palms of their hands, or have genital problems, including soreness, redness, or a variety of skin irritations. To repeat: there are *no* known medical problems associated with masturbation.

Can a person masturbate too often?

This question is asked all the time, and it is impossible to provide a specific answer estimating how many times a person can masturbate. If given a figure, some people may misunderstand and take that number as a standard for what is permissible or recommended. Masturbation is an individual matter. However, if someone finds that normal activities are disrupted by thinking about or engaging in masturbation, it might be helpful to talk with a family physician or counselor.

What is a French kiss?

Kissing with the lips closed is a traditional kiss. Kissing with the lips and mouth open and the tongues involved is a French kiss. It may be called a French kiss because the French have a reputation for being amorous. Sometimes it is also called a deep kiss or soul kiss.

What is a hickey?

Some people find it enjoyable to suck or gently nip their partner — often on the neck, breast, or thigh. A red mark or bruise may develop, and this is called a hickey. These marks are also called suck marks or monkey bites.

What is necking?

Kissing usually involves the face as well as the neck. "Necking" is a term commonly used to describe any extended kissing and hugging.

What is petting?

Petting is the step beyond necking. It includes feeling and stroking your partner's body, including the arms, chest, breasts, legs, and perhaps the genital area, either outside or inside the clothes.

Are necking and petting sexual activities?

Necking and petting definitely are sexual activities. Both necking and petting are often called "making out."

Are necking and petting dangerous?

Neither is physically harmful unless the situation gets out of hand, to the point that it gets rough or that two people get so sexually aroused that they have unprotected sexual intercourse, that is, without using a form of birth control.

Can a boy masturbate a girl and vice versa?

Yes. This is mutual masturbation. For some couples it can be a satisfactory substitute for intercourse, especially if one or both of the partners is unready, reluctant, or unwilling — for whatever reasons — to engage in intercourse. Some couples may engage in mutual masturbation when the female is menstruating. For unmarried young couples, masturbation, especially simultaneous masturbation, is preferable to engaging in unprotected intercourse. Female-to-male masturbation sometimes is referred to by the vulgar phrases "giving a hand job" or "doing a dry run." Male-to-female masturbation is commonly referred to as "fingering." Sometimes mutual masturbation is called "heavy petting."

What is foreplay?

Foreplay involves becoming sexually aroused by kissing, necking, and petting in preparation for sexual intercourse.

What exactly is sexual intercourse?

Sexual intercourse is the sexual joining of two individuals, sometimes called mating. In human sexual intercourse between a male and a female, the male's erect penis enters the female's vagina. They move together as the male pushes his penis back and forth inside her vagina, and she responds by pushing and moving against him. His back-and-forth motions, usually called strokes, and her responding pressure in pushing rhythmically against him are extremely pleasurable. These intense feelings are caused partly by friction on the sensitive head of his penis and on her sensitive clitoris. The resulting physical and emotional excitement can lead to orgasm, the climax or peak of pleasure. Orgasm occurs when he ejaculates his semen into her vagina and she has intense feelings because of the wave of rhythmic, muscular contractions in the sides of the vagina.

Are making love, having sex, and having intercourse all the same thing?

These expressions are three ways of referring to the physical act of sexual intercourse. Making love and having sex, however, can be used to refer to a variety of sexual activities not always including sexual intercourse.

What is the best position to use the first time a couple has intercourse?

It depends on what makes the individuals feel at ease and most comfortable. There is no right or wrong way to have sexual intercourse. Some positions may simply be more comfortable or convenient, given the couple, the situation, and the location.

Do all females bleed and have pain the first time they have sexual intercourse?

Neither bleeding nor pain is necessarily present during a female's first sexual intercourse, but experiencing either one or both is normal. If the hymen is broken or if it has been sufficiently stretched, it may not tear. When intercourse breaks a hymen, the tissue is torn or split and then flattens out as part of the vaginal wall. It may bleed a bit when torn, but bleeding and pain usually are slight. Tearing is the usual cause of bleeding and pain during and after first intercourse. Pain during sexual intercourse often is the result of tight vaginal muscles, caused by tensing up during intercourse.

At what point in sexual arousal is a female's vagina ready to have a penis inserted?

Usually the vagina is adequately lubricated (wet) after sufficient foreplay, the period of increasing sexual excitement that often includes necking and petting. If an overly eager couple attempts to have intercourse too quickly — without adequate time for foreplay — the couple may find intercourse difficult, painful, and unsatisfying.

Should a couple use lubricants before having sexual intercourse?

This is a personal choice. Some couples may find that intercourse is more comfortable and pleasant if they use a lubricant, others may find lubricants messy and a nuisance to apply. If they decide to use a lubricant, one made with a water base that dissolves readily, such as K-Y Jelly, is preferable. Prelubricated condoms and contraceptive foam, jelly, and cream also act as lubricants. Petroleum jelly should be avoided.

Can the vagina be too small for a penis to enter?

Entry may be difficult the first time a female has intercourse, and it may seem as if her vagina is too small; however, the normal vagina of a sexually mature female can expand to accommodate an erect penis, and it enlarges many times greater to allow for the passage of a baby during childbirth. If a female's vagina is so small that an erect penis cannot enter, she could have a very rare abnormality that needs to be evaluated by a doctor.

Is it important to know everything you are doing during sexual intercourse?

Knowing everything may, in fact, take away some of the excitement and romance. There is no prescribed or approved way of behaving during sexual intercourse. Many people are not even aware of all the things they are doing during intercourse. Being spontaneous, in fact, is desirable. It is, however, important to take birth-control measures to ensure that an unplanned pregnancy does not occur. In brief, it is important to know something but not necessarily everything.

Do positions have anything to do with enjoyment or the risk of getting pregnant?

There is a myth that having sex standing up will prevent pregnancy. That is false, because the force of gravity does not prevent sperm from making the journey toward the fallopian tubes. Different positions can enhance or detract from the enjoyment of sexual activity. Couples need to experiment and find out for themselves what are the most enjoyable or comfortable positions. Naturally, any position that is uncomfortable or painful should not be used.

How do people know if they are having sex the right way?

It is impossible to describe in detail just the right moves at the right time. There really isn't any patented guide to good sex in ten or twenty easy steps! For one thing, every person and every situation is different. The give and take of a relationship means the partners have to wait and see how things are developing and then respond and react to each other as honestly and openly as is comfortable. They have to improvise and experiment as they go along, whether they are experienced or just beginners. Partners need to communicate and to share both their knowledge and uncertainty since no one is 100 percent in control in any sexual situation.

Before starting any sexual relationship, a couple should try talking about what they want and how they feel about each other. Although many people may think that great sex has to do with the right physical positions and well-timed moves, most partners find that what is going on in their heads — expectations and feelings — leads to real pleasure and lasting happiness.

Why don't people always have orgasms during sexual intercourse?

There may be several explanations for why people don't always have orgasms during sexual intercourse. Some men can maintain an erection for an extended period of time without ejaculating during sexual intercourse. If a man is able to ejaculate by masturbating but not during intercourse, he should consult a physician or counselor.

For women, orgasm may not be experienced during every sexual encounter. As most men should know and all women do know, the female orgasm can be faked. Some men believe that intercourse is not complete or successful unless a woman has an orgasm. But a satisfying, healthy sexual experience is possible without a woman's having an orgasm every time. Demanding an orgasm every time, in fact, may spoil the experience for both partners. However, if a female is never able to achieve an orgasm during sexual intercourse, she may wish to consult a physician or counselor.

Why is it sometimes difficult for a woman to reach orgasm?

Some women have difficulty reaching orgasm for reasons that are not always clear. For some women, masturbation may be a more satisfying and easier way to achieve orgasm. For those females who desire orgasm in a sexual relationship, it can be helpful for the female to tell the male what she needs in the way of stimulation to achieve orgasm.

Can something be done to help both partners reach orgasm at the same time?

Simultaneous orgasm is overrated and unrealistic as a sexual goal, and this so-called ideal experience probably again reflects the American preoccupation with keeping score in sexual matters. Simultaneous orgasm usually occurs as a happy dividend of a satisfying sexual encounter, not as a conscious intention. If it happens, fine, and if it doesn't a couple should not get upset or discouraged.

The main consideration in human sexual relations is for a couple to achieve feelings of closeness and affection. Rather than striving for simultaneous orgasm, couples need to consider what sorts of physical and emotional help and encouragement they can give each other to increase mutual pleasure and intimacy.

What is the physical difference between a good and a bad sex partner?

This question implies that it is possible to judge an adequate or inadequate sex partner by some objective standard of physical skill or capability. In fact, assuming that both partners are in good health and have no special medical problems, they should be able to have good sexual relations. As always, the most important aspect in any ongoing human relationship is how well the people get along emotionally and psychologically.

Can frequent sexual activity cause physical harm to a person?

There is no evidence that frequent sexual activity can cause harm. Sometimes, however, frequent sex over a prolonged period of time can cause soreness, redness, and irritation to the genital area. In addition, if sexual activity involves several partners, then taking precautions against sexually transmitted diseases is essential (see Chapter 13, "Sexually Transmitted Diseases").

Can a man get "hung up" or stuck in a woman during intercourse?

No. The male loses his erection soon after ejaculation.

Can a penis harm a woman's cervix?

A normal cervix will not be harmed during sexual intercourse.

What is oral sex?

Oral sex is using the mouth to stimulate the genital area of the partner.

Is oral sex safe?

Oral sex is safe if neither partner is infected with a sexually transmitted disease.

What are fellatio, cunnilingus, and 69?

Fellatio (fe-LAY-she-oh), sometimes called by the vulgar terms "blow job" or "giving head," is kissing, licking, or sucking the male's penis.

Cunnilingus (cun-ee-LING-us), sometimes called by the vulgar term "eating out," is kissing, licking, or sucking the female's vulva, clitoris, and vagina.

Partners engaging in oral sex with each other simultaneously is called 69. The term refers to the position of the partners, because they lie in opposite directions, facing each other's genital region.

Do most people enjoy oral sex?

This is difficult to know for certain. Often one partner enjoys oral sex more than the other. The most important thing is for both partners to feel comfortable with their actions. A person should not feel pressured or forced into doing something he or she finds unpleasant.

What is anal sex?

Anal sex is the insertion of the erect penis into the rectum of the partner.

Is anal sex harmful?

Because bacteria are present in the human rectum, anal sex may be hazardous unless good hygiene is practiced by both partners. There is always a danger of transmitting bacteria from the rectum to the vagina. In some cases, anal sex can be a health risk because of the danger of passing sexually transmitted diseases, particularly acquired immune deficiency syndrome (AIDS), from an infected individual to a healthy one. (See Chapter 14, "AIDS.")

What is a vibrator, and can it be harmful?

A vibrator is a mechanical device, usually powered by batteries or electricity, that is used by females to stimulate the genital region, especially the clitoris. A vibrator can create the sexual excitement and orgasm associated with masturbation. A vibrator can be harmful if it irritates, bruises, or tears the tender tissues in the genital area.

What is a dildo, and can it be harmful?

A dildo is an object shaped like an erect penis, and is used to create sexual stimulation and excitement. Dildos can be made of various materials and lubricated to ease insertion. Using a rough or unclean dildo could be harmful because of the possible transmission of venereal diseases such as gonorrhea and chlamydia. (See Chapter 13, "Sexually Transmitted Diseases.")

At what age and under what conditions can two people legally have sex?

In most states there are laws specifying an age at which it is legal for a female to have sexual intercourse. Some states have what are called statutory rape laws; these prohibit having sexual intercourse with a female under a certain age (often fifteen or sixteen years old), whether or not she consents to the act. ("Statutory" comes from the word "statute," meaning "a law passed by an elected body," such as a state legislature.) These laws are intended to protect young women from being forced to engage in sexual relations before they are old enough to decide for themselves.

It is possible to find out whether there is a statutory rape law in your state by calling a family-planning clinic or a local teenage hotline.

In some states it is illegal to engage in oral or anal sex. These regulations are sometimes called sodomy laws. Such regulations may be aimed at forbidding or discouraging homosexuals from engaging in sexual acts. Some laws that restrict sexual freedom continue to be tested in courts of appeal around the country. There is also a federal law known as the Mann Act, which forbids taking a female under the age of eighteen or twenty-one (depending upon the state) across state lines for the purpose of having sexual relations.

What are the laws and punishments related to premarital sex?

In some states it is still against the law for anyone except married couples to have sexual intercourse. Such a prohibition is sometimes called a law against fornication. Although these laws remain in effect in some states, legal charges and prosecutions tend to be infrequent.

CHAPTER 10

CONCEPTION AND PREGNANCY

How does a female get pregnant?

A female becomes pregnant by having sexual intercourse with a male who ejaculates sperm into her vagina that fertilizes her egg.

What is conception?

Conception occurs when the fertilized egg becomes implanted in the uterus. The moment that this occurs marks the official beginning of a pregnancy.

What is ovulation?

Ovulation occurs when one of the ovaries releases an egg. Every month, complex chemical messengers called hormones stimulate the ovaries to release one egg. Before this happens, usually in the middle of the menstrual cycle, as many as five or six eggs are prepared but only one (occasionally two) is actually released. Under the influence of certain drugs a doctor may prescribe to overcome infertility (temporary inability to become pregnant), a woman may release multiple eggs.

Can a female tell when she is ovulating?

Some females whose menstrual cycle is regular — on a twenty-eight-day pattern, for example — know that they are going to menstruate on the same day each month, but this regularity is unusual. Females whose cycles are fairly regular can predict accurately when their periods will occur and on which day, if not at what hour, they will ovulate.

Some young women will know they are ovulating because they will have some discomfort — perhaps some lower abdominal cramps, perhaps some sharp pain — around midcycle (Day 15). This simply represents the egg being expelled from the ovary and traveling to the fallopian tube. There can be some very minor bleeding, just enough to cause some irritation of the lining inside the abdomen. For some women, this happens on a regular basis, and the discomfort signals the fact that they are ovulating. Discomfort at the time of ovulation, however, is not particularly common, and it is certainly not something that one can count on as a telltale sign that ovulation is occurring.

How and where does fertilization occur?

Sperm travel through the vagina, the cervix, and the uterus, and make contact with the egg as it moves down toward the uterus. This union usually occurs at the halfway point in the fallopian tube.

How much time is needed for fertilization to occur?

The time needed for fertilization varies. The egg usually remains alive for about one or two days. Sperm can live perhaps two to three days, at most, in the female reproductive tract, and sometimes that much time is needed for the sperm to travel to the egg, even though they can move fairly quickly. It is estimated that under favorable conditions sperm can move about an inch in less than ten minutes. About twenty-four to thirty-six hours usually elapse from the moment a male ejaculates in the vagina to the moment of fertilization. It could take place a little later, depending upon how long the sperm live.

How many sperm cells are needed to make a woman pregnant?

Of the hundreds of millions of sperm cells released in each ejaculation, just one sperm cell is needed to produce a pregnancy.

Can two sperm enter one egg simultaneously and fertilize it?

No, only one sperm can enter an egg. Once a sperm has made contact, that egg is sealed off from further contact, and another sperm cannot unite with it.

Why do men have an almost unlimited supply of sperm but women have only a certain number of eggs?

At birth, a female with two normal ovaries possesses as many as 400,000 microscopic eggs, some of which will be released during her menstrual cycles and have a chance to be fertilized. In each ejaculation a man has 300 million to 500 million sperm — what sounds like an ocean of sperm in comparison to the single egg! However, no man has an unlimited supply of sperm. The number of sperm can vary in each ejaculation. A man's age, physical condition, and health can affect his sperm production temporarily or permanently. (See Chapter 19, "Infertility/Sterility.")

Because the journey up the vagina, through the uterus, and into the fallopian tube is long and difficult, an enormous number of sperm are necessary to improve the chances of just one encountering and uniting with the egg. Of course, for one reason or another, many of the sperm never complete the trip up the female reproductive tract.

Does a woman ever have a shortage of eggs?

A normal female will not have a "shortage of eggs." There may be times during her reproductive years when she is unable to ovulate. During pregnancy, for example, women do not release eggs. In addition, a medical problem, emotional stress, an eating disorder, weight loss — all can prevent ovulation. Usually these problems can be corrected. There are, however, some serious diseases of the ovaries that interfere with or prevent the production of eggs. Fortunately, these problems rarely affect teenagers.

How old does a female have to be before she can become pregnant?

The minimum age depends on when the female reaches puberty. It can vary quite a bit, from as young as eight to as old as seventeen. A female cannot get pregnant before she reaches puberty, when her ovaries start to enlarge, breasts start to develop, pubic hair begins to grow, and hips begin to widen. In this earliest stage of puberty, most girls do not ovulate (that is, their ovaries do not release eggs), so they cannot become pregnant.

Can a female become pregnant before she has her first menstrual period?

Some girls begin to ovulate — usually without knowing it — before they start having periods. If that happens, a girl might incorrectly believe that because she has not had her first period, she cannot get pregnant. Although it is rare, a young female can, in fact, become pregnant just as she begins ovulating.

Can a female get pregnant the first time she has sex?

Yes, a female certainly can get pregnant the first time she has sexual intercourse. More often than you would imagine, young females have intercourse only once without using contraceptives and become pregnant. Young teenage females who are midway in their sexual development and are ovulating regularly have a good chance of getting pregnant. Older teenagers have an even greater chance since they undoubtedly are ovulating.

Many teenagers believe that, because the chances of getting pregnant might not be great at any one time, it simply could not happen to them. Obviously, this is very risky thinking.

Can a woman get pregnant without actually having intercourse?

It is impossible to become pregnant without having sperm meet egg, so some type of union is necessary. Of course, this union can be arranged through artificial insemination or a procedure called in vitro fertilization. (See Chapter 19, "Infertility/Sterility.") Aside from special methods of fertilization, pregnancy occurs following sexual intercourse, when the sperm travels through the reproductive tract of the female and meets the egg, usually in the fallopian tube.

There are females who insist that they never had intercourse, yet they became pregnant. It is highly unlikely that a female could get pregnant without having actual penetration of the vagina, but many women worry about this happening to them. During intimate, passionate encounters, partners are not always aware of the exact position or movement of the penis. A female may believe she was not penetrated — that the male's penis did not enter her vagina — when, actually it did, possibly for just a few seconds. If momentary penetration occurs, even in the outer portion of the vagina, some leakage of semen is possible, and the sperm may migrate up the vagina to the cervix and into the uterus. Despite the high odds against this happening, fertilization can occur.

Can fingers transfer sperm into a female's vagina?

Sperm could be carried accidentally on the fingers or other part of the hands from the penis to the vagina. Partners should always be careful about letting any sperm get near the vagina.

Can a woman get pregnant if her partner ejaculates on her thigh or stomach?

If ejaculation takes place outside the vagina, it is impossible for the sperm to migrate into the vagina from the abdomen or any other place. Even if sperm come in contact with the labia, right at the entrance to the vagina, the possibility of fertilization is small unless sperm enter the vagina or the penis penetrates the vagina slightly.

Can a woman become pregnant even if her partner pulls out his penis before he ejaculates?

Yes. Some females believe sexual intercourse really has not happened because their partners practiced withdrawal. That is when the male inserts his penis into the vagina but withdraws it before he ejaculates — a practice called coitus interruptus. Ejaculation takes place outside the vagina. But even in these cases, a female can become pregnant, because some semen containing sperm often leaks into the vagina before withdrawal. Also, when a male first has an erection, a bit of semen escapes. This first seminal fluid is clear and sticky and serves as a kind of lubricant. This substance contains some sperm — certainly enough to fertilize an egg. The seminal fluid ejaculated at climax is thick and milky and contains a higher concentration of sperm.

At what stage in the menstrual cycle is a woman most likely to get pregnant?

Think of a menstrual cycle as lasting approximately twenty-eight to thirty days, and count the first day of the period as Day

1. The most likely time to get pregnant would be between Day 10 and Day 20 of the cycle, because ovulation would be expected from Day 13 to 17.

Sperm usually remain alive in the female reproductive tract for two days, perhaps three or four days at most. If a woman has sexual intercourse a few days before ovulation, the sperm may remain alive within the female reproductive tract long enough to fertilize the egg released from the ovary. The egg takes up to four days to travel through the fallopian tube, but it is only viable (capable of living) for a day or two after it is released.

What are the safest times for a woman to have intercourse without getting pregnant?

Women, especially young women, just are not regular enough in their menstrual cycles to be able to predict precisely enough when they are ovulating and when they are "safe." Unexplained factors such as emotional or physical stress or an infection might interfere with ovulation. Or the cycle may be perfectly normal but ovulation may not always occur exactly on Day 15. So it is quite unwise to consider the rhythm method (having sex only during so-called safe times) as an effective form of birth control.

Can a female get pregnant if she has intercourse during her period?

A female is *less* likely to become pregnant by having intercourse during the time of menstrual flow, but pregnancy is *possible* nonetheless.

If a young woman's hymen is intact, can she still become pregnant?

Yes. All females have a hymen — a ring of tissue at the entrance to the vagina. Obviously, menstrual flow takes place through the hymen. If fluid can get out of the vagina, fluid can get into the vagina.

Rarely, females have total obstruction of the hymen. Blockage of the vagina is a rare medical condition that can be corrected by surgery.

If a female does not use birth control, what are her chances of getting pregnant?

The chances of becoming pregnant for healthy people having frequent sexual intercourse are very high — probably 90 percent or higher.

If a female does not feel any sexual desire during intercourse, can she still get pregnant?

Yes. It is not necessary for a female to feel any pleasure or to have an orgasm in order to become pregnant. What counts is human physiology — how the body works.

Is it true that a female cannot get pregnant if she has intercourse on top of the male, or standing up, or in the shower?

Position has nothing to do with it. What matters is penetration of the vagina by the penis. This can occur in a variety of positions. Although it might seem that in certain positions the force of gravity would cause most of the semen to run out of the vagina, in reality this does not happen. What is essential is penetration, with or without ejaculation. It takes just one sperm and one egg to produce a pregnancy.

Can a female get pregnant from French, or deep, kissing?

No.

Can a female get pregnant by having oral sex?

No, it is not possible to get pregnant by having oral sex. Some teenagers think a female can get pregnant from swallowing sperm, but that is simply untrue.

If a woman is already pregnant and has sex, can she get pregnant a second time?

No, this cannot happen, because a woman does not ovulate during pregnancy.

Does a male ever have a "safe" period?

No. Most males are fertile throughout their adult lives. As a matter of fact, even if a male is able to have intercourse four or five times in the course of twelve hours, the fourth or fifth time he has intercourse he is just as likely to produce sperm that can result in a pregnancy as he was the first time. Multiple ejaculations do not necessarily reduce the sperm count, nor does masturbating before having intercourse.

There is no evidence of any particular time or any cycle when a man might have a higher sperm count. There probably are times when he is less fertile — if he gets sick or has had some infection such as mumps, for example. By taking a hot bath or shower, a man may reduce his sperm count very slightly, but this reduction is temporary and insignificant.

If a male is able to have an erection, is it always physically possible for him to make a female pregnant?

It depends on other functions of his reproductive organs being normal. He must maintain the erection. He must also produce sperm. Neither the thickness, volume, or color of a male's semen (the ejaculated fluid, a mixture of sperm and seminal fluids) is an indication of how many sperm it contains. Only by examining semen under a microscope can a sperm count be made.

Young boys can have erections but cannot produce sperm until puberty. A man who has had a vasectomy (an operation chosen by a male who does not want to risk having his sexual partner become pregnant) produces sperm, but they are not present in the semen that he ejaculates.

Does the size of the penis determine the number of sperm ejaculated?

We are size-conscious about many things. Males seem to think that penis size is important. Penis size, in fact, has nothing to do with number of sperm. Sperm production requires normal testicles, not a large penis.

Is it true that sperm die when or if they are exposed to air?

Yes, they die after a few hours. If sperm are collected for artificial insemination, they are frozen immediately.

Are some women more likely to have multiple pregnancies?

If one or both of the partners is a twin or triplet, the couple has increased chances of having multiple births. Females who are being treated for infertility may take fertility drugs that increase their chances of having multiple births.

Are females who take birth-control pills more likely to have twins, triplets, or larger multiples of children?

No. If a female uses birth-control pills properly, the risk of pregnancy, single or multiple, is reduced to less than 1 percent. (See Chapter 11, "Contraception.")

What are the different types of twins and what causes twins to occur?

Fraternal twins result when a female releases *two eggs* during a particular month and both are fertilized by separate sperm. These fertilized eggs, when implanted in the uterus, are separate (they have separate placentas and yolk sacs — their sources of food) and they get along as individual fetuses (the unborn babies). Fraternal twins can be of the same or opposite sex, and their chromosomes (basic units of heredity) are different.

Identical twins, however, come from *a single egg* and a single sperm. During the very early stages of cell division, while the fertilized egg is becoming an embryo (a baby in its earliest stages of development), it splits into two separate fertilized cells, each with identical chromosomes, which then grow in the uterus as two embryos. Identical twins share a single placenta because they begin as the union of one egg and one sperm.

How can a female tell if she is going to have twins?

An ultrasound examination produces a television image of the uterus, created by the visible echoes of sound waves. An ultrasound of a pregnant woman usually can reveal the number of fetuses as well as the number of placentas. The doctor also may be able to hear multiple heartbeats through a stethoscope.

Do twins result from two episodes of intercourse?

A woman could conceive twins following two different episodes of intercourse. If the woman releases two eggs, both eggs could be fertilized after separate sexual episodes. The result would be fraternal twins. If the woman had different sexual partners, then fraternal twins might be conceived, and each twin might have a different father.

Can a couple plan to have twins?

It is impossible to plan to have twins. It is true, however, that women who take fertility drugs to increase the likelihood of pregnancy tend to have more multiple conceptions — followed by multiple births — than other women.

How do triplets occur?

Triplets, which occur much less frequently than twins, may result if three eggs are released and each is fertilized by different sperm. These triplets would be fraternal because each would contain different chromosomes. It is possible to have a combination whereby two of the babies are identical twins and one is fraternal. It is possible, although rare, to have identical triplets, all having grown from the division of a single egg. Most often, triplets are identical twins plus a fraternal brother or sister.

What are Siamese twins?

Siamese twins are created when a single sperm fertilizes a single egg and then during cell division the two embryos do not separate completely. As a result, the twins are joined at the abdomen, hip, chest, or, sometimes, even at the head. They may share some internal organs, such as the liver or digestive tract. Sometimes they can be separated successfully with surgery. The term "Siamese twins" comes from Chinese twins, named Chang and Eng, who were born early in the nineteenth century in Siam (which is now Thailand).

Does the mother or the father determine the sex of the baby?

The father determines the sex of a baby. Males have two sex chromosomes (carriers of genetic material) called X and Y. Females have two sex chromosomes, called X and X. Each sperm cell carries either an X or a Y chromosome, and each egg carries an X chromosome. During the fertilization process, there are two possibilities: (1) If a sperm containing an X chromosome from the father fertilizes the egg, the baby will be female (XX = female);

or (2) If a sperm containing a Y chromosome from the father fertilizes the egg, the baby will be male (XY = male).

Is there any way to increase the chances of having a girl or boy?

For centuries couples have been trying to find ways to select the gender of their children. Many studies and experiments have been performed to learn if it is possible to influence the sex of the baby: what positions in intercourse are used, what the partners eat or drink, whether a woman experiences orgasm, how often and at what time of the day or night intercourse occurs, and so on. But, as yet, there is no scientifically accurate or reliable way of planning or influencing the sex of the baby. Myths, theories, and hopes, however, persist.

There is no scientific explanation as to why the children in some families are mostly female and others overwhelmingly male. Conception and determination of gender occur at that "magic moment" when sperm unites with egg.

How many teenagers get pregnant each year in the United States?

The teenage pregnancy rate in this country rose substantially for many years but recently has steadied, and even declined slightly. Despite this, the United States has one of the highest teenage pregnancy rates among Western nations. Approximately 10 percent of all females aged fifteen to nineteen get pregnant each year. This means that more than 1 million teenagers aged fifteen to nineteen become pregnant every year in the United States. And each year an additional 30,000 girls younger than fifteen get pregnant. It is estimated that more than one-third of all teenage girls in the United States become pregnant at least once before reaching the age of twenty.

How many teenagers have babies?

Three out of ten teenage pregnancies end in abortion; one out of ten ends in miscarriage. The remaining six out of ten pregnant teenagers — about 600,000 each year — who have their babies face health risks during pregnancy and delivery that are much higher than those for adult women. Unfortunately, their babies are at increased risk of being born prematurely, of having low birth weight, and of dying during infancy.

Why is the teenage pregnancy rate so high?

I can think of at least four factors that have contributed to the high rate of teenage pregnancy. These include the ways teenagers react to changing attitudes, take risks, and attempt to prove their sexual capability, and the fact that they may choose abortion as an option.

- *Reacting to changing attitudes:* Most teenagers today are aware of changes in sexual attitudes and values. They know that in many ways this is a less restrictive society, more accepting than that of fifty years ago.

- *Taking risks:* Certainly, most adolescents behave responsibly, but a large number of teenagers still are willing to gamble when it comes to sex — and other activities as well. During the teenage years, many young men and women adopt an "It can't happen to me" attitude. They need to show that they are stronger, smarter, and less likely to get hurt by their own actions or those of others.

One of the motives prompting some teenagers to play the roulette wheel about getting pregnant — "Is it the 'safe' time of the month to have sex?" — is an unconscious desire to find out whether everything "works properly." Or, a young woman may want to prove that she is mature enough to have children.

When a pregnancy occurs, a young woman may be thinking, "Well, I wasn't sure that everything was normal, but now I know that I'm OK." For her, getting pregnant confirms that she has a normal reproductive tract. She may be very unhappy about being pregnant, but at least somewhere she has tucked away the information that she is not infertile. She may feel that she has proclaimed that she is a woman, not a child. In many cases, pregnancy for a young woman may be understood as success: "I can have something that belongs completely to me."

- *Proving sexual capability:* As for young men, they are usually not concerned so much with the idea of infertility (inability to reproduce) as with being able to prove their manhood and maturity. Most of the male problems with sexual activity take place above the neck. In addition, at one time or another, all males fear that they may not be able to perform. That particular issue can lead to many difficulties.

For a variety of reasons, a young man may not be ready for a sexual experience but may be forced into a situation because of peer pressure or through the advances of a young woman. Then, because of uncertainties about his own sexuality, he is unable to maintain an erection and have sexual intercourse. This failure to perform, even once, can cause great concern and worry. Impregnating his partner thus "proves" his manhood.

• *Having the option of terminating a pregnancy:* Although teen-agers know that contraceptives usually are easy to obtain and can make sexual activity much less risky, they do not always use them. This is because some believe contraceptives interfere with sexual pleasure or are inconvenient. In addition, young men and women realize that, as a final option, they may be able to choose to have an abortion. This, too, is a more accessible choice than it was twenty years ago. (See Chapter 12, "Abortion.")

CHAPTER 11

CONTRACEPTION

What is contraception?

Contraception deals with the science and methods of preventing conception, that is, preventing pregnancy. It is also referred to as birth control. Strictly speaking, the most effective way to prevent pregnancy is to practice abstinence — avoiding sexual intercourse or other sexual activities that may introduce sperm into the vagina.

Who should be responsible for contraception — the man or the woman?

Preventing pregnancy needs to be a shared responsibility between male and female. By mutual agreement, after careful consideration, the partners should decide who will take responsibility for contraception.

BIRTH-CONTROL DEVICES AND PRODUCTS

What is a condom?

Condoms sometimes are called prophylactics (pro-fa-LACK-tix), something that prevents or protects, because they can prevent pregnancy as well as protect against the male's giving or receiving a sexually transmitted disease during sexual intercourse. Condoms, also called rubbers or safes, are sheaths, shaped like the finger of a rubber glove, which fit over the erect penis. They can be made of very thin rubber, often latex, or from the very thin tissues of animals such as sheep. A condom may be lubricated to help ease intercourse, and it may have a small pocket at the end to hold the semen. Because a condom stretches so easily, it can fit an erect penis of any size.

How does a condom work?

A condom is designed to trap semen and prevent sperm from entering a female's vagina. A condom also is intended to protect against infection, especially sexually transmitted diseases. The proper way to put on a condom is by carefully rolling it down over the erect penis, leaving some room at the tip to hold the semen. It should be carefully removed after ejaculation to make sure no semen leaks out.

How effective is a condom?

A condom is about 95 percent effective when used alone — and correctly — as a method of contraception. It is about 98 percent effective when used in conjunction with special foams or creams that kill sperm.

Is a condom safe to use?

A condom is quite safe. In fact, it is one of the safest and least complicated forms of birth control.

What are contraceptive creams, jellies, and foams?

Contraceptive creams, jellies, and foams are spermicides (sperm-killing substances) that are inserted into the vagina soon *before* sexual intercourse. Contraceptive foam is a light, airy cream that resembles shaving cream. These spermicides, which coat the lining of the vagina, are applied with a small plastic inserter. It is important to read and carefully follow directions for using these contraceptives to ensure effectiveness.

How effective are contraceptive creams, jellies, and foams?

If they are used in conjunction with a condom or a diaphragm (described later in this chapter), they can be up to 98 percent effective. Used alone, they are not considered reliable contraceptives. Some types of creams, jellies, and foams contain a substance that protects against sexually transmitted diseases.

Are contraceptive creams, jellies, and foams safe to use?

Contraceptive vaginal creams, jellies, and foams have been tested extensively and have proved safe, nonirritating, and effective when used in conjunction with a condom or diaphragm.

What is the pill?

The birth-control pill is a prescription drug for women specifically designed to prevent an unwanted pregnancy. The pill usually contains both of the hormones (estrogen and progesterone) necessary for menstrual flow to occur.

How do birth-control pills work?

The pill works by interfering with the pituitary hormone called follicle stimulating hormone (FSH), which causes ovulation (release of an egg from the ovaries each month).

How is the pill used?

Many varieties of birth-control pills are taken for twenty-one days, then stopped for seven days, during which time the menstrual period usually occurs, and then taken for another twenty-one days. Other varieties are taken for twenty-eight days, and the last seven pills are drug-free and have no effect.

When does the pill become effective?

The pill becomes effective as soon as a female has completed the first twenty-one days of taking it.

How effective are birth-control pills?

If used properly, the pill is a very effective form of contraception. The pill is effective more than 98 percent of the time if taken exactly according to schedule. (If a sexually active young woman misses taking the pill for more than three days, she should use another method of contraception.)

Is the pill safe to use?

Research and years of successful use indicate that the pill is safe, especially for nonsmoking younger females who have no major health problems.

What are the pill's side effects?

There are no dramatic side effects of the pill unless it is used by a person who smokes or has a history of severe headaches, circulatory problems, or high blood pressure. The birth-control pill is not recommended when any of these conditions apply because side effects, although rare, can be serious. Slight weight gain, breast tenderness, and bloating also may accompany the use of the pill. These problems ordinarily would not be serious enough to discontinue taking the pill.

There are a number of birth-control pills, differing in the specific mixture of hormones. Each young woman who wishes to take the pill must be evaluated by a doctor before a particular pill is prescribed.

Will a teenager's parents have to know if she decides to go on the pill?

Parental involvement and knowledge are sensitive issues that require agreement between patient and doctor. Young women who want to go on the pill can do so without their parents' knowledge or permission. Confidentiality between patient and doctor cannot be broken without the patient's consent. However, it is usually in the best interest of the teenager to discuss birth control and other sexuality issues with her parents.

What is a diaphragm?

A diaphragm is a flexible ring that is covered with rubber and fits over the cervix, the mouth of the uterus. The diaphragm is an obstacle or barrier that prevents sperm from entering the cervix. The principle is the same as that of the condom, which a male uses to prevent sperm from entering the vagina and migrating toward the cervix and uterus. The diaphragm also serves to hold spermicidal cream, jelly, or foam up against the cervix.

How effective is a diaphragm?

When properly inserted and used with a spermicidal jelly, cream, or foam, a diaphragm is from 95 to 98 percent effective. The spermicide is placed inside the diaphragm before it is inserted into the vagina. (Additional spermicide must be inserted into the vagina before repeating intercourse.) Using the diaphragm without the spermicide greatly reduces the effectiveness of this contraceptive method. To assure maximum effectiveness, the diaphragm must be fitted for the specific individual by a doctor or nurse practitioner.

Is a diaphragm safe to use?

A diaphragm is entirely safe to use and may be an acceptable method of birth control, particularly for a female who has infrequent sexual relations. This method of birth control, however, does require some advance planning, and proper insertion may take some practice. The diaphragm should remain in place at least six hours after intercourse, but to reduce the risk of infection, it should never be left in place longer than twelve hours. A diaphragm can be used when a female is menstruating. Because it blocks menstrual flow, however, it should be removed six to eight hours after intercourse.

Can the man or woman feel the diaphragm when it is in place?

During intercourse it would be quite unusual for either partner to be aware of the presence of a diaphragm.

Can a woman take a shower or bath right after intercourse if she uses foam and a diaphragm?

Yes. The water will not interfere with or dilute the effect of either contraceptive method.

What is the vaginal sponge?

Vaginal sponges are soft discs resembling dimpled powder puffs. The sponge contains the same spermicide used in most contraceptive creams, jellies, and foams. When inserted into the vagina, the sponge kills sperm, absorbs sperm and seminal fluid, and may serve as a barrier to the cervix.

The sponge is less effective than the diaphragm at preventing conception, presumably because it is not fitted to each female's vagina. Because of doubts that health professionals have about its effectiveness and the possibility of infection, the vaginal sponge is not recommended for use by young women.

What are vaginal suppositories?

A vaginal suppository is a capsule containing spermicidal jelly or foam designed for insertion into the vagina before sexual intercourse. Once it is inside the vagina, the suppository coating melts, and the sperm-killing jelly or foam is intended to cover the walls of the vagina and the cervix.

How effective are vaginal suppositories?

Used alone, vaginal suppositories are about 96 percent effective in preventing pregnancy. When used in conjunction with a condom, the effectiveness rate rises to 98 or 99 percent.

Are vaginal suppositories safe to use?

Although vaginal suppositories are safe and can be convenient, this contraceptive method alone is not recommended. Used with a condom, however, this method is both safe and effective.

What is an IUD?

An IUD (intrauterine device) is a small specially designed object that a physician inserts in the uterus to prevent an unwanted pregnancy. An IUD remains in the uterus for extended periods of time, up to a year. IUDs are hooked or twisted in shape and are made from a variety of materials, including plastic and metal. When inserted properly, IUDs are very effective in preventing pregnancy.

How does an IUD work?

An IUD is intended to prevent a fertilized egg from implanting itself in the wall of the uterus and developing into a baby. Exactly how and why an IUD prevents this process from happening is not fully understood.

What are the side effects of an IUD?

Among the side effects of using an IUD are vaginal discharge, pain during menstrual periods, occasional bleeding, or a general feeling of abdominal discomfort. Because of the potential problems that IUDs cause, this form of contraceptive is not desirable or recommended for most females, especially young women.

What is a cervical cap?

A cervical cap is a rubber contraceptive device that is inserted into the vagina to cover the cervix and serve as a barrier against sperm. It can be worn for a short length of time or left in place for several weeks. Cervical caps are designed to permit menstrual flow.

To assure its effectiveness, a cervical cap must be fitted with great care by a doctor. Because of the possibility of failure of proper fit or proper insertion, cervical caps are not recommended for use by young females.

What is the morning-after pill?

The morning-after pill is a hormone preparation containing estrogen and progesterone. It works by producing a menstrual flow that flushes away a possible fertilized egg following unprotected sexual intercourse. The morning-after pill really should not be thought of as a routine form of contraception, because prevention of unwanted conceptions should occur before, not after, a mutual decision is made to engage in intercourse. In some extreme cases, however, such as rape, the morning-after pill may be prescribed.

What are the best kinds of birth control for teenagers?

For people who have sexual relations infrequently, the recommended type of birth control would be for the male to use a condom while the female uses a sperm-killing cream, jelly, foam, or vaginal suppository.

If a female has sexual relations often, it is probably best for her to use the birth-control pill, which has a very high rate of effectiveness (about 98 percent) when taken according to schedule. The pill is also probably the best choice if the preparations required to use a condom and spermicidal agent are unacceptable to one or both partners.

Where can a person get birth-control supplies?

Contraceptive supplies requiring a prescription or special fitting (birth-control pills, IUDs, diaphragms, and cervical caps) usually are available at any family-planning clinic and at most community health clinics or from physicians, especially gynecologists, who provide this kind of information and assistance. Other contraceptive supplies, such as condoms, creams, foams, and sponges, are "over-the-counter" items usually available — and visible — in most drugstores. Drugstores often have self-service displays.

What are the laws about buying supplies?

Some states may still regulate the sale of contraceptive materials according to a minimum age. When information is needed, the local pharmacist usually can provide details.

Are contraceptives expensive?

Contraceptives need not cost much. Family-planning clinics can supply information about monthly costs for supplies for both males and females. Avoiding pregnancy need not be expensive, but being pregnant always is.

Do parents need to know if teenagers use contraceptives?

No. In our society young men and women traditionally have been reluctant to tell their parents about their sexual activity, especially their use of contraceptives.

OTHER METHODS — AND NONMETHODS — OF BIRTH CONTROL

What is the withdrawal method of birth control?

This is a practice used by the male of withdrawing his penis from the vagina before ejaculation occurs.

Can withdrawal prevent pregnancy?

Not reliably. In fact, it runs a high risk of causing pregnancy. Before withdrawal, the erect penis may leak some fluid containing sperm, which could fertilize an egg.

What is the rhythm method?

The rhythm method involves refraining from sexual activity during the time of ovulation. Ovulation usually occurs between Day 13 and Day 17 (counting the first day of menstrual flow as Day 1) of a female's menstrual cycle. Since sperm can remain alive in a woman's reproductive tract for several days, it is safest to avoid intercourse from Day 10 to Day 20. If she is always right on schedule, a female may be able to figure out which days are the safest. According to this particular strategy, any day is "safe" for sexual intercourse except those around the time of ovulation.

Is the rhythm method effective?

Despite the most careful planning and restraint exercised by both partners, statistics reveal that the rhythm method prevents pregnancy less than 50 percent of the time. The rhythm method works if — and only if — the female's cycle is right on schedule and sexual intercourse is never attempted on the unsafe days during ovulation. Teenagers, however, rarely have menstrual cycles that are regular enough to predict the time of ovulation.

What are the temperature and mucus methods?

Both the temperature and mucus methods are probably most often used by women who are trying to get pregnant, rather than by those interested in preventing conception. During ovulation a female's temperature goes up very slightly — perhaps by one-half to one degree. If she keeps a very accurate temperature chart during her menstrual cycle, a female will note the days during her cycle when her temperature is elevated and she can assume that she is ovulating. If she wants to get pregnant, a female's chances during those days obviously are much higher.

The temperature method is not usually recommended for young women because it requires such careful record-keeping, and even then it is easy to miscalculate exactly when the fertile days are occurring.

Vaginal and cervical mucus is thinner (more watery and less sticky) during the time of ovulation. If a female keeps a careful watch on the changing consistency of her cervical mucus, she will see indications of when she is ovulating — that is, when she is fertile and likely to become pregnant.

The mucus method is less reliable than the temperature method. Keeping track of the thickness of cervical mucus as a method of contraception is not recommended for young women.

Can plastic wrap be used instead of a condom as a contraceptive?

No. Using plastic wrap or any other "homemade" substitute for a condom almost guarantees leakage of some of the semen into or around the female's vagina.

Can a tampon be used as a form of birth control?

No.

Can feminine hygiene spray be used as a form of birth control?

No.

Is douching after intercourse a form of birth control?

No attempt to "clean out" the vagina following sexual intercourse is ever completely successful. Semen contains too many sperm to flush out and eliminate every single one.

Can Coke be used as a douche?

Neither Coke nor any other soft drink nor any chemical-containing substance should be used as a douche for purposes of contraception or feminine hygiene. The lining of the vagina is easily irritated by chemicals. The use of douches is unnecessary and not recommended for young women.

What is sterilization?

Sterilization is a surgical procedure that makes a male or female infertile, unable to start a pregnancy. In females, the procedure is referred to as a tubal ligation or hysterectomy. In males, the procedure is a vasectomy.

What is tubal ligation?

Tubal ligation (also called "having your tubes tied") is an operation in which a surgeon cuts and ties or seals off each of a woman's fallopian tubes, making it impossible for an egg to travel into the uterus. The female, therefore, cannot become pregnant.

Is tube-tying dangerous?

If performed under proper surgical conditions, the operation to tie the fallopian tubes is fairly simple and not dangerous.

Can tube-tying be reversed?

Reconnecting severed fallopian tubes is a difficult operation. Because of the uncertainty of successfully reversing a tube-tying operation, most females wait until they are certain they do not want to bear any more children before having this procedure.

Does having her tubes tied affect a woman's ability to have sex?

No.

What is a vasectomy?

A vasectomy (va-SEK-tuh-me) can be thought of as the male version of a female's having her tubes tied. The vas deferens, the two small tubes carrying sperm from the testicles to the urethra, are surgically cut and the ends sealed off. This usually is an uncomplicated operation that can be performed under local anesthesia in a physician's office.

Is a vasectomy dangerous?

Properly done, a vasectomy is not dangerous.

Can a vasectomy be reversed?

A vasectomy is difficult to reverse, and this procedure is rarely successful.

Does a vasectomy affect a man's ability to have sex?

A vasectomy has no effect on a man's ability to have sex because the operation does not affect the ability to have and maintain an erection or to ejaculate.

What is a hysterectomy?

Hysterectomy (hiss-tuh-REK-tuh-me) means removal of the uterus. A simple hysterectomy is the removal of just the uterus, leaving the fallopian tubes and ovaries. A complete hysterectomy is removal of all of those reproductive organs. Most surgeons make every attempt to leave one or both ovaries in place because of their very important function in producing the female hormones.

CHAPTER 12

ABORTION

What is an abortion?

"Abortion" is the term commonly used to indicate the interruption of pregnancy. "Abort" means "to terminate," and an effective abortion terminates a pregnancy. An abortion may be planned and intentional or it may be unplanned and spontaneous. When the pregnancy does not continue following fertilization of the egg, the result is a spontaneous abortion, also called a miscarriage. A miscarriage can be signaled by a heavy flow of blood from the vagina and may require medical attention. An intentional abortion often is performed by a physician at the request of a female who has become pregnant and desires to terminate the pregnancy. This sometimes is called a therapeutic abortion, because it may be intended to preserve health.

How is an abortion performed?

An abortion is usually performed by a doctor, preferably during the first three months of a pregnancy. One way is called the suction method, which involves attaching a suction device to the cervical canal and then suctioning out the contents of the uterus. This procedure can be performed with local anesthesia so that the female remains awake throughout. Another method is called a D and C, which stands for dilation and curettage. This involves enlarging (dilating) the cervix and then gently scraping (curetting) the lining of the uterus with a surgical instrument that resembles a spoon with a long handle. This method is usually not recommended for teenagers. Dilation and curettage may also be performed for reasons other than pregnancy. If an older woman has unusual bleeding, for example, a doctor may want to perform a D and C as a way to find out what the gynecologic problem may be. This procedure is intended to clean out the uterus and remove any material caused by disease, such as infection or a foreign growth.

Up to how many weeks of pregnancy can a female safely have an abortion?

The safest time for an abortion would be during the first trimester — the first three months (about thirteen weeks) — of pregnancy. Abortions performed during the second trimester are often much more difficult for the female and may involve complications and aftereffects. Under expert medical care, a young woman might consider a second-trimester abortion.

What are the advantages and disadvantages of abortion?

The question of abortion is a highly individual matter, based on personal judgment, background, religion, morals, and personal health. One obvious advantage of abortion is that terminating a pregnancy is sometimes necessary for health reasons. Another advantage is that it allows a female to postpone having a child. For example, a teenaged female who is not ready for the responsibility of parenthood might want to finish her education and prepare for a career. A disadvantage might be that the female may later regret not having the child. After an abortion some females find that sorrow and guilt over the lost opportunity to have a child are especially difficult to deal with.

Can any pregnant female have an abortion?

Any pregnant female could have an abortion under proper medical conditions.

How many abortions can a female have without affecting her ability to have normal pregnancies and births later?

It is impossible to state a specific number of abortions a female can have before she should be concerned about her ability to have a normal pregnancy and birth. Obviously, if a female wants to have children, repeated abortions only postpone the time of childbearing, and the older a female becomes the more difficult it may be to get pregnant and have a normal, uncomplicated birth. If a female has had multiple abortions, the medical procedures involved may interfere with her having a normal pregnancy and birth.

Are abortions painful or dangerous?

Abortions need not be painful, but they can be. With the use of modern medical procedures, doctors can eliminate most of the pain. Every attempt is made to keep the individual comfortable and free of pain. She almost always will experience some physical discomfort, such as cramps (caused by contractions of the uterus) and abdominal pain, for about twenty-four hours after the abortion. Abortions can be dangerous, even fatal, if not performed according to modern medical practice by qualified medical professionals under sterile conditions.

Can a female perform an abortion on herself?

No female should *ever* try to perform an abortion on herself. When such an attempt is made — by introducing a foreign object into the vagina, for example — the female usually harms herself and fails to bring about an abortion. Infection, possibly leading to blood poisoning, often is the result. An attempted abortion that leads to an infection is called a septic abortion.

Is abortion ever used as a means of birth control?

Some females who do not use contraceptives may resort to abortion as a means of birth control. Such a costly and often worrisome approach to birth control is certainly not recommended for anyone. Clearly, this misuse of abortion is hard on any female's reproductive system, and, of course, it is expensive.

Where can a woman go if she wants to have an abortion?

Deciding to have an abortion should always be done with help from at least one trustworthy person — sexual partner, friend, health professional, or parent. A family-planning clinic or health center can usually provide counseling. Pregnancy information services are usually listed in the yellow pages of the telephone directory, and making calls to obtain information about available services can be helpful. Staff members at authorized pregnancy counseling services respect and maintain the confidentiality of all individuals who make any kind of inquiry.

It is never safe to rely upon information obtained from anyone connected with an unlicensed or illegal abortion clinic or service, no matter who recommends it.

Do parents need to give their consent for their daughter to have an abortion?

In most states, minors must have the permission of their parents or guardians to obtain an abortion. In certain states it may be possible for "mature minors" to obtain such consent from a state agency without securing their parents' permission. Whether a young person is a mature minor is determined by a physician, possibly in consultation with the appropriate state agency. Legal advice about the availability of abortion services for minors usually can be obtained through family-planning clinics or the local health department.

Can a woman be forced by her parents or by her mate to have an abortion if she does not want one?

No. It is impossible and illegal to force any female to have an abortion. Whatever her age, every female has medical and legal rights protecting her from being forced to do anything against her will.

Does a pregnant woman have any obligation to tell the man involved before she has an abortion?

She does not have any *legal* obligation to inform the man involved. However, after weighing the factors involved, a female may feel a moral obligation to share that information, but that is a decision she must make for herself.

What is the average cost of an abortion?

It is difficult to make a general statement about the cost of any medical procedure in any area of the United States. Figures often cited by pregnancy information services are between $180 and $250 for an uncomplicated clinic abortion. Costs probably would be higher in a hospital.

What are the abortion laws?

Federal law guarantees every female the right to have an abortion. State laws, however, vary considerably concerning the age at which abortion can be performed without parental consent. It is likely, therefore, that some young females who want to have an abortion without involving their parents may have to travel to another state to undergo the procedure.

Should every female who has an abortion seek counseling?

It is strongly recommended that every female who has had an abortion, regardless of age, engage in some kind of counseling. Brief individual counseling with a qualified professional counselor may be satisfactory for some young women. Others may need and benefit from long-term counseling with a good therapist. This is an individual matter, but pregnancy information services can be helpful in locating a good therapist.

The male whose partner has had an abortion may want to participate in counseling with the female, or he may wish to seek counseling himself.

What is the best way to deal with the moral issues involving abortion?

This is an individual decision that each young woman needs to explore. Pregnancy information services, family-planning and health clinics, and religious organizations all can provide opportunities to discuss abortion-related issues and questions. Whether an individual will benefit from engaging in such considerations and discussions is a question each young woman must decide for herself.

Is it against all religions to have an abortion?

Individual religions view abortion differently. It is true that some religions disapprove of or forbid abortion. The question of the official position of any religious body is one that a young woman should discuss directly with her local church leader.

CHAPTER 13

SEXUALLY TRANSMITTED DISEASES

What does "venereal disease" mean?

"Venereal disease" (VD) is the popular name for any sexually transmitted disease — an illness spread through intimate sexual contact or activity. The word "venereal" comes from the name of Venus, the Roman goddess of love. The medical term for venereal disease is sexually transmitted disease (STD), which is more descriptive and is coming into more general use.

How do people get sexually transmitted diseases?

Sexually transmitted diseases can be passed along through a variety of sexual practices, including sexual intercourse, oral sex, anal sex, or any exchange of body fluids, especially semen, blood, or saliva. Some germs find a way into a person's bloodstream, usually through a break in the skin or membranes lining body openings such as the vagina, mouth, or anus. It is important to remember that only those people who are already infected with a venereal disease can transmit the disease to others.

Can sexually transmitted diseases be cured?

Many types of sexually transmitted disease are relatively easy to treat, especially in their early stages. Anyone who wonders or worries about whether he or she may be infected should see a physician without delay for a test and, if necessary, treatment.

What are the different types of sexually transmitted diseases?

There are many types of STDs, and none of them is either harmless or pleasant to live with. They are:

chlamydia infection
gonorrhea
yeast infection
trichomonas infection
venereal warts
genital herpes
pubic lice, or crabs
scabies
syphilis
acquired immune deficiency syndrome (AIDS)

What do the following words mean: "clap," "drip," "dose," and "infected"?

These are all slang terms associated with or used to describe sexually transmitted diseases. "Clap," "drip," and "dose" commonly refer to gonorrhea, which for years was the most common STD in the United States. "Infected" could refer to almost any STD but probably is connected most often with AIDS, chlamydia, gonorrhea, and syphilis.

What is the most dangerous type of STD?

The most dangerous type of STD is acquired immune deficiency syndrome (AIDS). It is fatal, there is no known cure, no truly effective treatment, and no vaccine to protect against its spread. (See Chapter 14, "AIDS.")

What is a chlamydia infection?

Chlamydia (kla-MID-ee-a) is the most common sexually transmitted disease. It is caused by a germ that is similar to a virus and is spread by sexual intercourse. There are a few symptoms of discomfort and difficulty in urinating for the male. There are seldom any noticeable symptoms for the female. She may experience some abdominal discomfort and vaginal discharge. Males experience discharge from the penis that may be a signal or clue to the presence of chlamydia infection. Once chlamydia is diagnosed, it can be treated quite easily with an antibiotic.

How long does it take for symptoms of chlamydia to appear?

The symptoms usually appear one to three weeks after infection.

What happens if chlamydia is not treated?

Females may develop pelvic inflammatory disease (PID, see below). Males can have infections of the urinary tract that recur until properly treated.

What is gonorrhea, and how is it caused?

Gonorrhea (gone-a-REE-a) is a sexually transmitted disease spread by intimate sexual contact, usually intercourse. Gonorrhea is caused by infection with bacteria called *n. gonococci,* from which the disease takes its name.

What are the symptoms of gonorrhea for the male, and how long does it take for symptoms to appear?

A male knows quite soon that he has gonorrhea. Extreme pain in the penis and difficulty in urinating are the most frequent problems. Males seek medical help as soon as these problems occur, which usually is within three to five days after intercourse with an infected partner. Gonorrhea can cause what sometimes is called "the drip," slow, painful dripping of urine mixed with pus instead of the normal easy flow of clear urine.

What are the symptoms of gonorrhea for the female, and how long does it take for symptoms to appear?

Gonorrhea infection often is without obvious symptoms in females. In fact, as many as 80 percent of females who have the disease experience no noticeable symptoms. There may be some slight pain or difficulty in urinating, and there may be an unusual vaginal discharge. In addition, there may be some pain in the affected areas of the body. The most common site for infection is the reproductive system — vagina, cervix, and uterus. The infection may also be present in the throat, anus, and urethra (the tube that carries urine from the bladder out of the body).

Symptoms develop slowly in the female. Generally, females find out about gonorrhea in the early and middle stages only if their partner tells them he has it. As a result, many females do not seek treatment until the disease has progressed to a damaging stage in which abdominal pain becomes severe because the fallopian tubes may have become infected.

Can gonorrhea be cured? If so, how?

Several types of antibiotics can cure gonorrhea. One major difficulty is that many types of gonococcus have become resistant to certain antibiotics. It often is necessary, therefore, to test the individual for sensitivity to particular antibiotics before starting treatment with the appropriate one.

What is PID (pelvic inflammatory disease)?

Because of infection of the female reproductive system, gonorrhea can cause severe, persistent abdominal pain, often accompanied by fever. This very serious problem is often referred to as PID. Chlamydia also can cause PID.

What is a yeast infection?

Yeast infections (candida albicans or monilia) are caused by a type of very tiny fungus and can be spread by sexual intercourse. Females may have a cheeselike discharge that can have a strong odor. Males may notice some inflammation of the penis. Both males and females may experience intense itching and skin irritation. Scratching the irritated area may cause a bacterial infection. Yeast infections are treated with prescription creams that are used in the genital area.

What is a trichomonas infection?

Trichomonas infection (sometimes called "trick") is a vaginal infection that produces a frothy vaginal discharge accompanied by itching and burning in the vaginal area. Many females have no symptoms. It is spread by sexual intercourse. Prescription medications are available to cure this condition.

What are venereal warts?

Venereal warts, which are caused by a virus, appear on the penis, especially around the head (glans). In the female, they appear on the labia and around the rectum. They look like any other unsightly warts that appear on hands or feet. The warts may cause itching and irritation. These warts can be treated, some with medicine applied directly to the area. A doctor can treat cases of extensive venereal warts and may decide to remove them surgically, sometimes with a laser.

What is genital herpes?

Genital herpes can be recognized by painful blisters on the shaft of the penis or in the vagina. It is transmitted by intimate sexual contact, usually intercourse.

How is genital herpes related to oral herpes (cold sores or fever blisters)?

Both illnesses are caused by members of a family of related viruses. Notice the term "related." The viruses are similar but not the same. The genital herpes blister resembles the cold sore that is typical of oral herpes. Genital herpes, however, behaves differently and requires different treatment.

Can genital herpes be cured? If so, how?

Genital herpes cannot be cured, although it can be treated to relieve the blisters and pain, which in time will disappear. The most common drug used for genital herpes is Acyclovir, which treats the acute illness but does not cure the disease. After the blisters go away, the virus is still present in the body, although it is inactive (dormant). The blisters, however, may reappear at any time in the future. Doctors estimate that genital herpes returns in about 75 percent of all males and females who have the disease.

Is it easier for males or females to tell whether they have genital herpes?

Genital herpes is more visible in the male than the female, but the female becomes painfully aware of her internal genital herpes sores during vaginal intercourse.

How does genital herpes affect males?

The effects are not usually disabling. The disease may interfere with a male's sexual activity from time to time when the blisters appear (or reappear) and need to be treated.

How does genital herpes affect females?

Genital herpes can be a problem because serious disease of the cervix can develop. The disease can be diagnosed in a gynecologic exam and treated.

Can genital herpes be transmitted when dormant?

Genital herpes probably cannot be transmitted when the disease appears to be healed (dormant, or in remission), but sometimes it can be difficult for a person to be absolutely certain that all signs and symptoms of disease have disappeared. If someone is uncertain about whether the disease is in remission, a doctor should be consulted.

What are crabs and pubic lice, and how do you get them?

Pubic lice, or crabs, are tiny insects that inhabit pubic hair, but are sometimes found in the underarms and scalp and on the chest. There are various forms of lice, such as head lice and body lice, and "crabs" is the slang term for the type that is found in the pubic hair.

The pubic louse lays eggs (nits), which become attached to the individual pubic hair shafts and hatch into lice. Pubic lice usually are associated with venereal disease. In addition to being transmitted during sexual intercourse, they can be picked up from the underwear and bed linen used by infected people.

All forms of lice can cause intense itching. Infections in the skin and the lymph glands may develop as a result of the scratching that follows. Lice can be treated with an application of an insecticide medication to the affected areas. Good hygiene and care in changing and laundering clothing can prevent recurrence of lice and crabs.

What are scabies, and how do you get them?

Scabies (SKAY-beez) may be associated with sexually transmitted disease, especially sexual intimacy between partners who have an STD. However, it is quite possible to pick up scabies without any sexual intimacy, for example, from underwear and bed linen used by someone who has the disease.

Scabies is caused by a tiny insect called a mite, which can get into the genital area and multiply rapidly. These mites burrow into the skin and can cause tiny lines to appear on the skin as they tunnel under the surface. Scabies usually causes irritation and itching. It can be treated with an application of an antimite medication to the affected area.

What is syphilis, and how is it caused?

Syphilis (SIF-a-liss) is a contagious STD caused by infection with a particular type of germ called a spirochete (SPY-row-keet). A spirochete has a spiral appearance under the microscope.

What are the symptoms of syphilis, and how long does it take for them to appear?

Syphilis begins ten to ninety days after intercourse with an infected partner as a painless, ulcerated (open) sore, called a chancre (SHANK-er), usually on the shaft of the penis or in the vagina. This sore contains the syphilis spirochete. The chancre lasts for up to a month and then, even if it is not treated, will disappear. However, without treatment the syphilis spirochete remains alive in the body. Then from one to six months later, secondary syphilis develops, which usually appears as a reddish-brown rash over the body. There may also be whitish mucous patches in the mouth and throat or in the vagina; hair loss; and swollen glands.

Most cases of syphilis are diagnosed and treated in the first or second stage. However, the second-stage symptoms also will disappear even if not treated, but the spirochete still remains alive and the disease will continue into a third, final stage.

Is it easier for males or females to tell that they have syphilis?

It is easier for a male to tell that he has syphilis, because of the visibility of the sore(s) on his penis. A female usually has no noticeable symptoms in the first stage, but may develop the rash in the second stage and brain and heart problems if the disease progresses into the third stage. A blood test is the simplest way of diagnosing the disease.

Can syphilis cause insanity?

Few people with syphilis in the United States today ever progress untreated to the final (third, or tertiary) stage, because treatment in early stages is successful. If, however, the disease progresses to the tertiary stage, syphilis can cause severe brain damage, and the resulting mental problems include insanity. About

25 percent of individuals with tertiary syphilis will develop paralysis, brain damage, or heart problems.

Can syphilis be cured? If so, how?

Syphilis can be cured with one of several types of penicillin. If there is any doubt about whether someone has syphilis, a blood test can be performed to make the diagnosis.

Is there a way to find out from whom you may have contracted an STD if you have slept with more than one person?

The best way to find out is to ask — as difficult or embarrassing as that may sound. It is the simplest and most direct method. People often are reluctant or ashamed to volunteer such information unless they are asked specifically.

How can a person avoid getting a sexually transmitted disease?

Using a condom will prevent transmission of most types of STD.

Does taking a bath or shower or douching after sex prevent sexually transmitted diseases?

No, these methods do not prevent STDs — or pregnancy.

Can a female be pregnant and have an STD at the same time?

It is possible to be pregnant and have an STD at the same time. That usually is a serious situation for the health of both mother and baby.

If a pregnant woman has a sexually transmitted disease, how will the disease affect the baby?

Each STD has the potential to produce medical complications for which the baby must be treated immediately after birth. The results for the baby will be very serious if the disease is syphilis or AIDS, because the baby could be born with severe physical and mental defects. Gonorrhea sometimes causes blindness in newborns.

Where are STD information and counseling available?

Counseling and information can be found in many places and from a variety of health professionals. Information should be freely available in all schools and libraries. The school nurse or doctor should have the latest information in pamphlet and book form. Some schools have health clinics for teenagers where counseling as well as information is available.

Family-planning clinics also offer a variety of information about STDs. The public health departments of all cities and towns should have information available, and doctors and other medical personnel on the staffs of these departments are ready to provide counseling.

Doctors in private practice can provide information and counseling to anyone with questions about an STD. Most hospitals can provide information about STDs through their community clinics and programs on public health.

Any person of any age who wants information, counseling, or an examination for STDs should seek help promptly. There is a national toll-free STD hotline available through the United States Public Health Service that can provide information and referral to clinics. The number is 1-800-227-8922.

If a minor goes for a test or receives treatment for an STD, will his or her parents be told?

All health organizations and medical personnel in the United States are required by law to keep confidential the names of all individuals, regardless of their age, who seek information, counseling, or examination. Parental permission is not needed for testing or treatment.

If you have any doubt about whether a medical professional or the staff of a particular health facility will keep your identity confidential, you should ask directly: "Will you keep my name and questions confidential? Who will have access to any written record of my contact with you?" If you are worried about the possibility of someone learning your identity or finding out what you are inquiring about, ask an adult you trust about the policy of confidentiality at that particular clinic or health facility. It is especially wise to ask someone who has a medical background or is familiar with the medical facilities and health resources in your community. If you are still worried, you can call the toll-free national STD hotline: 1-800-227-8922.

Do not let any question about sexually transmitted diseases go without getting a trustworthy answer.

CHAPTER 14

AIDS

What is AIDS?

AIDS (acquired immune deficiency syndrome) is a contagious infectious disease. (A syndrome is a group of signs and symptoms associated with a particular illness or disease.) It is spread through sexual contact, sharing contaminated needles, and receiving contaminated blood and blood products. Pregnant women who are infected with AIDS can pass the disease to their unborn children.

AIDS affects both homosexual (attracted to the same sex) and heterosexual (attracted to the opposite sex) individuals. The groups most often affected by AIDS are male homosexuals; males and females who have had many sexual partners, both homosexual and heterosexual; intravenous drug users; and hemophiliacs (individuals with a rare blood clotting disorder who require transfusions of certain blood products). These groups sometimes are called the at-risk groups.

What causes AIDS?

AIDS is caused by one member of a family of viruses called retroviruses, also known as human immunodeficiency viruses, or HIV. (A virus is any one of a group of organisms too tiny to be seen under an ordinary microscope. Viruses can cause infections in animals, including human beings. The common cold and measles are examples of illnesses caused by viruses.)

The AIDS virus attacks special white blood cells called T-lymphocytes, which help the body fight infections. When there is significant destruction of the T-cells, an individual cannot fight off most germs that invade the body. As a result, the body begins to develop infections, especially unusual and persistent ones that are difficult to overcome even with the best drugs and medical care. These infections often are ones that people with normal immune (defense) systems would never develop.

What is the immune system?

The immune system goes into action when the body needs to fight off germs, including bacteria and viruses, that can cause infection and disease. When germs find their way into the body, special white blood cells called B- and T-lymphocytes try to fight off these invaders. B-cells and T-cells are essential for the creation of antibodies, which help destroy germs. Also involved in the defense system are special blood cells called macrophages, which help the B- and T-cells destroy bacteria, viruses, and other germs.

When a person has a normal, healthy immune system, the body's automatic defenses search for and destroy almost all kinds of invading germs. People with AIDS, however, do not have normal immune systems. The AIDS virus attacks the T-cells in the blood, leaving the immune system ineffective in defending against invading germs.

What kinds of infections do people with AIDS develop?

One of the most common infections that attacks people with AIDS is a persistent, severe form of pneumonia (pneumocystis carinii). In addition, some people with AIDS develop rare forms of cancer and severe, progressively worsening disease of the nervous system and brain.

Can AIDS be cured?

There is no known cure for AIDS. Several experimental drugs are being tested that may prolong and improve the quality of life of individuals who have AIDS. There are drugs that can kill the virus but are unable to restore the immune system to its normal state. The ideal treatment would destroy the virus and bring the B- and T-cell lymphocyte levels back to normal. Scientists are searching for the drug(s) that would produce these effects. In the near future, research scientists hope to have a vaccine perfected that will prevent AIDS.

How long does it take for the AIDS virus to turn into the disease in someone's body?

AIDS apparently is a relatively new health problem. The first cases of AIDS in the United States were diagnosed in the late 1970s and early 1980s. If a person's antibody test for AIDS is positive, it means that person has been *exposed* to the HIV virus. Of those people who test positive for the presence of the virus, 10 percent who have no symptoms of the disease will eventually develop the disease, and 25 percent of those with symptoms will develop the disease within three years. It is expected that these percentages will increase in the future.

Is AIDS always fatal?

When the disease becomes active, that is, when symptoms become obvious — showing that the immune system can no longer fight off infections — there is no treatment yet known that can prevent death.

How long do people with AIDS have to live?

From the beginning of obvious symptoms and the accompanying illness, people with AIDS usually live from eighteen to twenty-four months. More effective drug treatments may extend the life expectancy of those with AIDS.

What is ARC?

AIDS-related complex (ARC) is a less severe form of AIDS. The major symptoms are fever, diarrhea, weight loss, and night sweats (excessive perspiration during the night, often to the extent that pajamas and bedclothes become drenched). ARC is also associated with reduced numbers of T-cell lymphocytes, those white blood cells that fight germs. About 25 percent of people with ARC will develop AIDS within three years.

Do more males or females get AIDS?

AIDS affects many more males than females. The number of females with the disease is rising, however.

Can babies, children, or teenagers get AIDS?

Yes, every age group can get AIDS. Babies get it primarily through birth by an infected mother, children through sexual abuse and possibly transfusions, and teenagers through intravenous drugs and unprotected sexual activity.

Is AIDS spread through anal intercourse; oral sex; vaginal intercourse?

Anal intercourse is the most hazardous sexual practice. The partner receiving semen infected with the AIDS virus may contract the disease. Cells of the rectum and colon may be infected by the semen, or the virus may enter the bloodstream through tiny tears in the lining of the rectum during anal intercourse.

Oral sex is the next most hazardous practice, with the partner receiving any body fluid from an infected partner running the risk of contracting the infection, possibly through an ulcer in the mouth, a crack in the gums, or an unnoticeable tiny split in the lip.

Increasing evidence shows that vaginal intercourse can present a risk if one person receives any body fluid from a partner who is infected with the AIDS virus.

Is it true that only gay men but not gay women can get AIDS?

Gay (homosexual) women who use intravenous drugs or who are bisexual (sexually active with females and males) may get AIDS. The AIDS virus is often spread by the use of unclean (contaminated) hypodermic needles. It would be possible for a woman who has sexual relations with both men and women to contract the disease from a male who had previously contracted AIDS from either a male or female with the illness.

Can a person get AIDS by kissing someone who has the disease?

It may be possible to contract AIDS through deep, open-mouthed (French) kissing with someone who has the illness, although the virus is rarely found in saliva. Currently, it is presumed possible to transmit the virus by exchange of saliva in deep kissing, although there is as yet *no proof* that it actually happens.

How can a person get AIDS from a blood transfusion?

The virus may be in the blood that is donated. However, very effective precautions are now taken to prevent blood or blood products infected with the AIDS virus from being used by any blood bank.

Can a person get AIDS by having a vaccination or a penicillin shot?

It is almost impossible for an injection of any kind to transmit AIDS — if it is performed under proper medical conditions. Needles in hospitals and physicians' offices are used only once and then discarded. A contaminated needle that has already been used by or for someone with AIDS could transmit the virus.

Can mosquitoes and other stinging insects spread AIDS?

This question, which is under investigation, has not been completely resolved. Currently, it is believed that an insect bite will not transmit the AIDS virus.

Can someone get AIDS by drinking from the same glass or same fountain or using the same toilet seat as a person with AIDS?

No. Today the most common ways of transmitting the illness are through intimate sexual contact and the use of contaminated hypodermic needles.

Can AIDS be spread through tears?

No.

Can people get AIDS by having their ears pierced or getting tattooed?

Yes, it is possible if the needle used for piercing or tattooing is contaminated with the AIDS virus.

Can children get AIDS from their parents?

Casual personal contact will not transmit AIDS to children. However, an infected mother can transmit the AIDS virus to her baby before or during the birth process. An infected mother or father might possibly infect a child through sexual abuse.

Can a person get AIDS from doing artificial respiration on a person with AIDS?

Mouth-to-mouth breathing as part of artificial respiration with a person who has AIDS might be hazardous. Whether the disease could be transmitted this way is still being studied.

If there is someone in school who has AIDS, should other students stay away from that person?

Not at all. Ordinary daily contact does not spread the AIDS virus.

Should people do anything special when they are around a person with AIDS to keep from being exposed to the virus?

Do not engage in sexual activity with that person.

Should everyone take an AIDS test? Would test results be given to a minor's parents or school?

Universal testing for AIDS is a controversial subject that has both scientific and legal complications to be studied and debated. Matters still to be resolved regarding the use of the test include confidentiality, the errors produced by current methods of testing, and interpreting the results.

After someone tests positive for the AIDS virus, what signs show that the person really has AIDS?

There are the ARC symptoms (fever, chills, night sweats, diarrhea, and weight loss), which show that the person is reacting to the AIDS virus. AIDS may be diagnosed when the individual develops pneumonia caused by a particular type of bacteria called pneumocystis carinii, a germ that ordinarily would not cause pneumonia in a healthy person. A person with a positive HIV test and symptoms of ARC who develops a persistent cough must be suspected of having pneumocystis carinii pneumonia. A diagnosis must be made by a doctor using the proper scientific techniques and tests.

How can a person tell if he or she has AIDS? Are the tests foolproof?

A doctor must make the diagnosis. The tests are not foolproof, and if there is any question about whether someone has AIDS, a doctor should be consulted.

Does everyone who tests positive for the AIDS virus develop AIDS?

No. Currently, 10 percent of those who test positive but have no symptoms will develop ARC, and another 25 percent who test positive and have some symptoms will develop AIDS. These percentages may become greater unless effective drugs and a vaccine are developed to combat the illness.

Is there any way to know for sure that a potential sexual partner does not have AIDS?

No. The only way that someone might be able to know would be if both partners exchanged information honestly concerning the possibility of AIDS having infected either one.

What is "safe sex"?

The safest sex is when both partners are free of the AIDS virus. "Safe sex" refers to the recommendation made by public health authorities that a condom should be used for all intimate sexual activity when there is any doubt about both partners being healthy and free from disease.

Are condoms 100 percent effective in preventing AIDS?

Nothing offers foolproof protection, but the use of condoms during sexual activity, including foreplay, is strongly recommended. An undamaged condom provides a barrier through which body fluids that may carry the AIDS virus cannot pass.

Do diaphragms help protect against AIDS?

No.

Does "safe sex" always work?

Remember that during intimate sexual contact there is *no* foolproof defense against being infected by someone with AIDS or who may have been exposed to AIDS. Obviously, a condom will help. So it probably is more accurate to say "safer sex" when talking about sensible precautions during sexual activity.

Are there special hospitals for people with AIDS?

Finding suitable hospitalization for people with AIDS has become a major public health problem in the United States. There are hospices (special homelike residences for people who have terminal diseases) in which individuals with AIDS can be cared for during the final stages of their illness. There are a few hospitals in the United States devoted exclusively to the care of people with

AIDS and ARC. These facilities are located in areas with large populations of AIDS and ARC patients. In addition, many large hospitals, especially research hospitals, are well staffed and properly equipped to care for AIDS patients.

Who can people talk to if they have private questions about AIDS, and will their privacy be protected?

Confidentiality is a delicate, often difficult matter. Care, caution, and thought should be exercised before confiding in anyone who is not fully informed about AIDS and the issues involved, or who may not be completely trustworthy. A trusted family doctor or public health nurse practitioner might be a good choice. He or she may refer the person to other professionals as needed. A person also can talk to an AIDS counseling or support group in the community or call the nearest one in the area. There are also informational hotlines. Anyone who phones the national hotline provided by the United States Public Health Service, toll-free, 1-800-342-AIDS (2437), is assured full confidentiality. The counselors who answer hotline questions can also provide referrals for further information and personal assistance.

CHAPTER 15

SEXUAL IDENTITY

Does sexual identity involve more than simply having the physical characteristics and features of a male or a female?

Yes, it certainly does. Sexual identity involves a highly complex set of factors — physical, emotional, psychological, familial, environmental — that combine to form an individual's internal and external sense of self.

What do "homosexual" and "heterosexual" mean?

"Homosexual" refers to males or females who are sexually attracted to people of the same sex over a significant period of time. (The Greek word *homos* means "same.") Most homosexuals take part in sexual activity with partners of the same sex and usually are not attracted to people of the opposite sex. "Heterosexual" refers to males or females whose sexual preference over time is for members of the opposite sex. (The Greek word *heteros* means "other" or "different.")

Are people born with their sexual preferences?

It is doubtful anyone knows the answer to this question. Endocrinologists (scientists who study hormones and other human biochemical substances), geneticists (scientists who study heredity), and psychologists (scientists who study human emotions and behavior) are attempting to find an answer, but no definitive explanation is on the horizon.

Do people keep their sexual preferences for their entire lives?

Whether people keep their sexual preferences for their entire lives depends to some degree upon the individual involved. This is a topic that continues to be studied.

What are the causes of homosexuality?

We do not know why humans develop as either heterosexuals or homosexuals. There are many theories that take either a hereditary or an environmental approach to sexual identity, meaning that it might either be inherited or be the result of certain influences in a person's life as he or she is growing up. Some theories try to show that sexual preference stems from a combination of heredity and environment. No one is certain of the answer. Homosexuality is *not* a disease; it is a matter of sexual preference.

What does it mean to be gay?

"Gay" is a descriptive term meaning "homosexual." It more often is used in referring to homosexual males, but homosexual females (also called lesbians) may be referred to as gay.

What percentage of the population is gay?

About 6 to 8 percent of the population is thought to be homosexual, or gay. Many experts on the subject of sexual preference, however, are not certain whether this estimate is accurate.

Are there more gay males than gay females in the United States?

Surveys indicate that there are more gay males than gay females in the United States. Whether those surveys accurately reflect people's sexual preferences is difficult to know.

How can a person figure out if he or she is a homosexual?

You do not "figure out" if you are homosexual. There are no universal or foolproof guidelines to identify homosexual or heterosexual individuals. You may get some indications by the way you think or fantasize about people of your own sex or the opposite sex. Sexual fantasies may occur when you see other people's bodies in a locker room or at the beach. Or they may occur without any prompting while you are studying or running or brushing your teeth. Adolescents normally have many vivid fantasies about both sexes before coming to a clear understanding about their preferences.

It is quite common for males and females to have concerns about homosexuality and to wonder about their own sexual identity. It is only through the slow process of sexual growth, development, and experience, however, that an individual gradually learns and recognizes personal sexual preferences.

Should anything be done if a person thinks that he or she is homosexual?

First, it is important not to treat the subject of homosexuality as if it were an abnormality or a disorder. Homosexuality is as legitimate a sexual identity as heterosexuality. It is not something to "do something about."

For some people it may be a good idea to discuss feelings and concerns with a respected, trusted adult — perhaps a teacher, a counselor, or a relative. It is important for this adviser to deal with all ideas and feelings in a confidential manner. Such a conversation is not designed or intended to direct or change feelings and thoughts. It is an opportunity to express and explore ideas and feelings. Talking to someone can dispel fears, calm any uneasiness, and provide useful, objective information that can help someone understand what homosexuality is about.

Do homosexuals look and dress a certain way?

It is a mistake to think that homosexuals, male or female, look or dress a certain way. It is impossible to tell if someone is a homosexual (or heterosexual) by appearance. When together in a group, some homosexuals may share certain characteristics, mannerisms, or styles with their friends, but that could be said as well about many groups of heterosexuals.

Is it a sign of homosexuality if once or twice a person fooled around with someone of the same sex?

No. Sexual experimentation often occurs while people are growing up and maturing, and a few casual encounters with someone of the same sex would not ordinarily be considered a sign of homosexuality. These experiments might include hugging, embracing, kissing, and perhaps masturbation. If these activities occur once or twice or even a half-dozen times, they would not indicate a homosexual preference. This kind of experimentation may happen at any time, but overall, it probably is more common among people of college and young adult age.

Is it a sign of homosexuality if a person is attracted to someone of the same sex?

Simply being attracted to someone of the same sex should be considered quite natural, an important part of the process of growing up and finding out how you feel about sexuality. Friends often will show physical affection, which is in keeping with their emotional attachment and attraction to each other. It is always important to have a trusted friend of the same sex — someone you feel comfortable with and with whom you can talk about almost anything without having to worry about watching your words or wondering whether what you say will be kept strictly confidential. Such displays of caring and affection should not be interpreted by others as signs of homosexuality.

Is it a sign of homosexuality if a person is eighteen and still a virgin?

This is a situation that males worry about much more often than females. Some people have expressed the opinion that if a male has not had sexual intercourse with a female by the time he is eighteen then he might be a homosexual. There is absolutely no basis for this opinion. It is perfectly fine to be a heterosexual male and still be a virgin at eighteen — or any age, for that matter — and not have to worry or wonder about your sexual identity or capability.

Is it a sign of male homosexuality if one testicle is lower than the other; a boy seems feminine or a girl seems masculine; a boy has lots of male friends but is not attracted to girls?

- It is very common for males to have one testicle — usually the left one — positioned slightly lower than the other in the scrotum. This fact of normal anatomy is not an indication of homosexuality.

• Calling a boy "feminine" can be a cruel blow to any young male in the same way that calling a girl "masculine" can hurt a female's feelings. Boys who prefer activities (perhaps supposedly nonathletic activities such as the arts, theater, and dance) that may not appear superficially to be "masculine" should not be tagged with what is intended to be an uncomplimentary label. People may point to a male's body language (including his posture or how he walks), manner of speech, clothing, or hair style and make unflattering comments or jump to unwarranted conclusions. The same goes for labeling a girl "masculine" who happens to engage in vigorous contact sports or likes to dress in unisex clothes or wears her hair very short and straight.

People often are concerned without good reason about homosexuality. Many tend to label as homosexual boys who have what they consider feminine traits or girls who have masculine ones. It is important to remember that "masculine" and "feminine" are subjective terms; they mean different things to different people. Everyone should be very cautious about making blanket statements regarding a particular boy's or girl's sexual identity or preference. Such characterizations hurt boys' and girls' feelings and allow stereotypes to persist among both males and females who should know better.

• It is very risky to generalize about a boy's sexual preference or identity on the basis of how many boyfriends or girlfriends he has. Whether he feels any attraction to girls is a subjective judgment and can change quickly depending upon the situation and the girl involved. This same caution would apply to making generalizations about a girl's sexual preference on the basis of how many girlfriends or boyfriends she has.

Some individuals have homosexual feelings that are never expressed. Others have homosexual feelings that are expressed or acted out in behavior toward others of the same sex. During adolescence, most homosexual feelings of males and females remain unexpressed even if strongly felt.

If a girl is a tomboy, is she likely to be gay?

Not at all. For a young girl in elementary or junior high school, being a tomboy usually means preferring what are thought to be traditional boys' activities and forms of dress. If a young girl happens to be a tomboy, that preference has nothing to do with whether she is likely to be gay later on.

It is impossible to know what a female's sexual preference is without understanding her situation and her feelings about others of the same and the opposite sex. A muscular, rugged-looking female who dresses in masculine-type clothes may unkindly be referred to as a "lezzie," "dyke," or "butch," regardless of what her true preference and identity happen to be.

How do homosexuals make love?

Homosexuals experience the same intensity of feelings and the same need to express affection and be intimate with another human being as do heterosexuals. Homosexuals make love in many of the same ways that heterosexuals do: by touching, caressing, fondling, masturbating, and engaging in oral and anal sex.

Isn't making love something only heterosexuals can do the right way?

There is no "right way" to make love. It is inaccurate to define or restrict making love to sexual intercourse involving a penis and a vagina. Homosexuals express their affection and make love in their own ways.

What is bisexuality?

Some individuals are sexually attracted to both males and females. They are able to find sexual pleasure and gratification with both males and females. They are called bisexuals. Bisexuals may have difficulty deciding whether heterosexual or homosexual activity is more appealing. Bisexuals often marry and have children, but occasionally they may seek out a sexual encounter with a member of the same sex. It is thought that more males than females are bisexual, but there is still little reliable information on this subject. Perhaps 5 percent or less of the adult population might be classified as actively bisexual, that is, having sexual relations with both sexes during the preceding year.

What does "coming out" mean?

"Coming out" is a male's or female's public declaration of a homosexual or bisexual identity or preference. A similar expression is "being (or coming) out of the closet." Open declarations of sexual identity have become more common and accepted in recent years as American society has become more accepting of varying kinds of sexual preference.

What should a "straight" person do if approached by someone of the same sex?

A "straight," or heterosexual, person should make it clear in a thoughtful, honest manner that homosexual behavior is not what he or she is interested in. The most direct, persuasive word, of course, is "No," said quite early in a conversation. What else needs to be said or explained depends upon the particular person and situation.

If a young boy or girl is approached by an older male or female, the best strategy is to say "No" firmly and to repeat it if necessary. If the older person persists, the boy or girl should seek help or simply leave the company of the older person as quickly as possible. If the approach or advance is made in public, the boy or girl should say "No" clearly and loudly enough to attract the attention of others. This usually will discourage the older person.

What is a transvestite?

The term "transvestite" usually refers to a male who dresses and tries to behave like a female for emotional or sexual gratification. It also can be used to describe a female who dresses and tries to behave like a male.

What is a transsexual?

"Transsexual" is the term used to describe a male who has undergone a sex change operation in order to assume a female body and identity. Such an individual, of course, retains the masculine chromosomes that he inherited from his parents.

What happens when a person has a sex change operation?

For emotional and psychological reasons, there are a small number of males who desire to change their sexual identity and become females. They may then undergo a sex change operation in which the male sex organs, penis and testicles, are removed, and through surgery they are provided with an opening similar to a vagina. These men are then given female hormones, which will produce feminine characteristics, including some small development of breast tissue. If breast development through hormone treatment fails, some men may choose to have plastic surgery to produce artificial breasts. Whether such sex change operations actually satisfy males is open to question and is being studied. Sex change operations to make a female into a male are rare and extremely difficult.

What is a hermaphrodite?

"Hermaphrodite" (her-MAF-ro-dite) means "part male, part female." (The name refers to the Greek god Hermes and the goddess Aphrodite.) The term, therefore, is sometimes used to describe people who are born with genitals and other characteristics of both sexes. Other descriptive terms for this condition are "ambiguous sexuality" or "inappropriate genitalia," referring to some mixture of sexual characteristics.

How do people become hermaphrodites?

Individuals are born with inappropriate genitalia; they do not choose or decide to take on some of the genital organs of the other sex, except in the rare case of a transsexual.

Can a hermaphrodite be cured?

A person born with inappropriate genitalia can undergo surgery to improve or eliminate the condition. In addition, hormone therapy may be necessary to stimulate development of certain male or female characteristics.

What is a eunuch?

A eunuch (YOU-nuk) is a male who has had his testicles removed. In other words, a eunuch is a castrated male. In earlier centuries, some gifted male singers either chose or were forced to become eunuchs. They were castrated before puberty to preserve their fine soprano voices, and they were called castrati. Also, many years ago, in some Oriental societies, male slaves were castrated so that they posed no sexual threat to the females in a harem.

CHAPTER 16

VARIATIONS IN SEXUAL BEHAVIOR

What is a prostitute?

A prostitute is a female or male who provides sexual services for money or other compensation.

Do the terms "whore," "call girl," "hooker," "tart," and "streetwalker" mean the same as a prostitute?

All these are slang terms for female prostitutes.

What is a "john"?

A "john" is a prostitute's customer, the individual who buys her/his sexual services. The term usually refers to a male.

What is a voyeur? Is it the same as a peeping tom?

A voyeur (voy-YOUR), a French term meaning "someone who looks," is a person who gets sexual pleasure or who becomes sexually excited by looking at other people who are engaged in sexual activity. A voyeur also may get a sexual thrill by spying on people who are getting undressed or whose nudity or near nudity suggests that they may be preparing for sexual activity.

A peeping tom is a voyeur who enjoys being secretive and sneaky. Peeping toms watch or spy on sexual activity, either close up by approaching someone's bedroom or at a distance by using binoculars or a telescope.

What is "flashing"?

A person, almost always a male, who exposes his genitals to strangers in public for the shock value is called a "flasher."

The term "flashing" comes from the practice of such an individual who opens his coat, unzips his fly, or drops his pants very briefly in public to allow an unsuspecting passerby to see a "flash" of his genitals. As soon as the flash is over, the flasher usually leaves quickly. Flashing can happen at almost any time in any public location. Some flashers prey upon children and adolescents, choosing them perhaps as a way of silently inviting them to sexual activity.

What is sado-masochism?

A sadist (SAY-dist) likes to hurt other people. A masochist (MASS-oh-kist) likes to be hurt or punished. The pain involved may be physical, psychological, or both. A sado-masochist is someone who enjoys punishing and being punished, often in a sexual situation. Spanking, whipping, and being bound or tied are just a few of the painful activities practiced in sado-masochistic sexual encounters.

Violent sex is sometimes described as exciting. Is this dangerous?

It often is said that intense feelings of pleasure and pain are closely related. Because violence usually means inflicting bodily harm, it is difficult to consider "exciting" (meaning pleasurable) any activity, including sex, that could cause harm or pain to another person. Violent sex, which could involve inflicting pain by means of the body or with "sexual implements" such as whips, spurs, handcuffs, ropes, or chains, can be dangerous and humiliating and cannot be recommended for anyone of any age.

What is pornography?

Pornography is writing, pictures, television, or any other form of communication that depicts people, most often females but sometimes males and children, in erotic (sexually arousing) poses or engaging in bizarre or perverse sexual activity — deviating from what is considered healthy and normal.

Is reading or looking at pornography harmful?

If reading or watching pornography actually stimulates or motivates people to socially or sexually aggressive behavior, it must be considered harmful.

What effect does pornography have on people of different age groups?

In many cases, pornography seems to have very little effect on adults other than to stimulate or mildly provoke sexual feelings for a brief time. Adolescents might be excessively stimulated if they read or look at pornography repeatedly or for extended periods of time. As far as children are concerned, pornography is unsuitable, inappropriate, and potentially harmful. No child should be exposed to any type of pornography.

Whether exposure to pornography harms an adolescent or adult depends upon the emotional health and strength of the individual. Parents who are concerned about the potential harmful effects of pornography might want to discuss the subject objectively with their adolescent children as a way of honestly conveying their personal views and values.

Will watching pornographic movies or reading pornographic material make a person promiscuous?

In all likelihood, watching pornographic movies or reading pornographic literature will not make a person promiscuous (prone to engage in sexual activities with many partners). Even though pornography may show or describe wild and unrestrained sexual activity, there is little evidence that people try to imitate such behavior. Saying this, however, is not a recommendation that anyone, especially teenagers, watch pornographic movies or read pornographic books or magazines because, in addition to repeated, explicit sexual activity, many "X-rated" films and pornographic materials depict aggressive, violent behavior directed at females.

What is a nymphomaniac?

"Nymphomaniac" is a term used to describe a female who may appear to have an appetite for sexual activities, especially sexual intercourse, that is never satisfied. Nymphomania should be considered a major emotional problem. Sometimes the term is used casually to "put down" a sexually active female, but using such a damaging label almost always is inaccurate and unfair.

Is it possible to have sex with more than one person at a time?

Yes, it is possible to have sexual activity with more than one person. Obviously, one can have sexual intercourse with only one person at a time, but it may be possible to be engaged in other intimate sexual activity at the same time with another partner.

What is a ménage à trois?

"Ménage à trois" is a French term for any combination of three people involved in sexual activities (literally, "a household of three").

What is a "gang bang"?

A "gang bang" usually refers to sexual intercourse in which a female has sex with two or more males in succession. Gang bangs are often associated with rape.

Is it possible for a person to have sex with an animal?

It is physically possible for human beings, both male and female, to have sexual relations with certain animals. This practice, called bestiality, sometimes is associated with farm animals. Obviously, unnatural sexual relationships cannot be encouraged or approved, even as an experiment.

CHAPTER 17

RAPE, SEXUAL ABUSE, AND INCEST

What is rape, exactly?

Rape is a physically violent sexual act against another person. Rape is usually committed by a male, who attempts to have sexual relations with another person, usually a female, against the other person's will. The sexual contact may be penetration of the vagina, anus, or mouth; ejaculation in the general area of the vagina or elsewhere on the body; or forcing the victim to engage in some other kind of sexual activity.

Rape almost always is associated with actual physical harm or the threat of harm to the victim, in addition to forced sexual contact. Victims usually feel that their safety and their lives are threatened unless they agree or yield to the sexual demands. Health professionals who care for rape victims usually find indications of physical force and violation. Physical force may be indicated by cuts, scratches, bruises, or other marks on the victim's body, especially in or around the genital area.

If a woman initially agrees to sex, but then decides she does not want to have intercourse and is forced into it, is that rape?

Rape is understood to be forcible sexual contact against a person's will or in spite of his or her protest. In a situation where there is disagreement about what actually happened during the course of a sexual encounter, it may be necessary to have a neutral third party, such as a judge or jury, decide what the facts are and which partner's version of the event is more believable or accurate. Both medical and legal evidence, which includes physical and emotional signs that violence was inflicted, may have to be evaluated before a decision can be reached. One of the reasons that many states have "age of consent" laws is to try to protect young women from being forced to have sexual experiences before they are old enough to know what they are agreeing to.

What should a female do if she is raped?

The most important thing a female should do if she is raped is to get help immediately from a reliable, trustworthy person — a member of her family, a friend, a member of the police department. She needs company — a companion whose emotional support she can absolutely depend upon.

For purposes of personal health and to protect legal rights, she should go as quickly as possible with this support person to the emergency room of a large hospital, neighborhood health clinic, or private doctor's office.

She should *not* change clothes, take a shower, or in any way clean herself up or take care of any injuries until a health professional sees and examines her. Rape victims often feel an overwhelming urge to get clean and remove any visible sign of the attack. It is very important, however, that all evidence of what happened remain as undisturbed as possible until she is assisted by someone with professional authority who is qualified to observe and evaluate her condition.

Her physical and emotional condition must be examined, documented, and recorded by qualified health professionals who can, if necessary, testify in court about the extent of her injuries. Doctors and nurses follow a special medical routine called a rape or sexual abuse protocol that is designed to check every type of physical and emotional injury that might be inflicted during a rape or an attempted rape. Their findings, gained through examination and conversation, make up the official medical and legal record.

The rape victim will find that health professionals who deal with sexual violence are exceptionally sensitive and sympathetic to what she has been through. She will be treated with great care and respect. Confidentiality will be maintained and her privacy will be protected. Nothing said or done during medical or legal evaluation will be made known to anyone other than those involved in the follow-up care or in the official investigation of the attack without the consent of the rape victim.

For everyone who goes through a rape examination, which is an emotionally demanding experience, counseling and emotional support are provided by a person specially trained to deal with rape victims and their particular problems. This counseling begins while the rape examination is going on and continues for some time afterward.

If a female who has been raped does not immediately report what happened, does not get professional help, and does not have her physical and emotional injuries properly attended to, it often turns out to be very difficult later on to convince medical and legal authorities that she actually was attacked. Therefore, it is important for anyone who is the victim of a sexual attack to get help quickly and rely upon a support network of family members and health and legal professionals to provide the kinds of short- and long-term help that are needed during the course of recovery.

How is a case of rape proved?

Rape can be investigated by having the victim go as quickly as possible to a hospital, clinic, or private doctor where a very detailed, specific medical examination is performed to try to determine exactly what happened. Both discussion with the victim and a medical examination are carried out to estimate the extent of injury and obtain needed evidence that could be used when the case is brought to court.

Evidence of rape could include signs of physical injury, such as bruises, scratches, or bleeding, or other damage to the vagina, hymen, or anus that indicates forcible entry or penetration; the presence of semen in or on the body; the presence of disease organisms as shown by laboratory cultures and blood tests. If a possibility of pregnancy exists, a female may be given a hormone pill to prevent the implantation of a fertilized egg. Tests may be performed to check for pregnancy and the presence of sexually transmitted disease.

What are the rape laws?

Rape laws vary from state to state, but in general they are very severe, and breaking these laws is considered a major crime, involving a charge of felony. If the offending male is identified and caught and there is sufficient evidence against him, a felony charge leads to a criminal trial. A male who is found guilty of committing rape almost always is sentenced to jail for a prescribed period of time, often more than one year.

What is statutory rape?

Some states have laws (statutes) that forbid sexual intercourse with any female below a certain age, usually fifteen or sixteen. If a male has sexual intercourse with a female below the legal age in a state that has such a statute, he may be charged with statutory rape even if the female agrees willingly to the act.

What is "date rape"?

"Date rape" occurs when a female agrees to go out with a male but that male forces her into having intimate sexual activity against her will. It is estimated that in three out of four rapes the female knows the male who attacks her. Date rape may occur because the male misunderstands how much physical intimacy his partner has agreed to or because he deliberately takes advantage of the situation and the trust his partner has placed in him. When alcohol or drugs are involved in a date rape situation, it may be very difficult to determine how much of what occurs is the result of misunderstanding, force, or the influence of drugs or alcohol on the two people.

Can a woman charge her husband with rape?

In most states a woman can bring a charge of rape against her husband if he forces her to have sexual intercourse against her will. Because a couple is married does not mean that the husband is "entitled" to sexual intercourse whenever it pleases him. A woman can charge her husband with rape, but she may have a difficult time proving her case and getting others to accept her version of what happened. She must be willing to go through the standard rape examination procedure and be willing to go through a trial.

Can a female rape a male?

It is physically possible for a female to rape a male, that is, to force him to have sexual intercourse with her against his will.

Although it can happen, there probably are few cases where a woman has been charged in court with such a crime by a man. Occasionally, an older female who is entrusted with a younger male's care may be accused of having made sexual advances to him, thereby abusing his trust.

Can a person rape someone of the same sex?

Rape by a person of the same sex is possible. A female may sexually abuse another female against her will. It may involve masturbation or oral-genital contact. A male can rape another male by forcibly introducing his penis into the partner's rectum to have anal intercourse, or he may abuse his partner through masturbation or oral-genital contact.

What can a female do to lessen the risk of being raped?

Every female should take advantage of opportunities to learn about rape. As an adolescent she should have an opportunity to attend a class or workshop conducted by experienced, sensitive teachers and counselors in a school, community clinic, or rape crisis center so that she can learn about self-protection and how to reduce her own risk of being harmed.

These instructional sessions usually involve information about being on guard and being alert to where and when sexual attacks most often occur. They provide suggestions about how to keep out of potentially dangerous situations. Such sessions often concentrate upon the need to be with someone when traveling in unfamiliar places. They emphasize how important it is to think ahead defensively to avoid getting into situations where the female is dependent upon strangers for assistance, protection, or transportation. Other topics of importance for self-protection may include how to behave with strangers; what to do in unfamiliar situations; when to yell for help; and how to escape from dangerous situations.

How is "sexual abuse" usually defined?

"Sexual abuse" is similar in meaning to "rape." It often is discussed in terms of the sexual mistreatment of young children by adults. Abuse occurs when a male or female child has had some type of sexual encounter with an adult or an adolescent who is significantly older and sexually mature or knowledgeable.

The abuse may consist of:

- *exhibitionism* — posing children in suggestive positions or taking pictures or films of children who usually are naked or partially clothed and encouraging them to engage in actual or simulated sexual activities. Exhibitionism may also involve an adult's exposing his or her genitals to a child as a way of exciting or enticing that child to further sexual activities.

- *voyeurism* — watching or spying on people in hopes of seeing them engaged in sexual activity, or encouraging children to engage in similar behavior. A person who does this is often called a peeping tom.

- *fondling* — touching or stroking the child's genital organs, buttocks, breasts, or other private parts of the body, or entering the vagina, rectum, or mouth with the mouth or fingers of the adult. Fondling may also involve an adult's encouraging or forcing a child to touch, stroke, or manipulate his or her genitals, perhaps to the point of masturbation.

- *intercourse* — forcing the child to engage in genital or oral sex or other inappropriate sexual acts, including fondling.

For teenagers, sexual abuse usually involves a sexual encounter that may include forcible entry into the vagina, rectum, or mouth with the penis, mouth, or fingers. It may involve genital or anal contact by the adult, or forcing the teenager to engage in oral sex or other inappropriate sexual acts, including feeling or fondling of the genital area or breasts. It may be difficult for a teenager to prove sexual abuse or unwanted sexual attention if these activities are confined to feeling or fondling.

What should a person do if he or she feels sexually abused by a parent, sibling, or another person?

It is very important for a person of any age to report sexual abuse to a trusted adult. If one parent is the abuser, that trusted adult might be the other parent, an aunt, an uncle or cousin, a close family friend, a doctor, a teacher or school counselor. If a sibling is the abuser, the same adults could be approached, beginning, of course, with the parents, who would be the most immediately concerned. If another person is involved, especially a stranger, the parents should be told first, and they then can report the incident(s) to the proper authorities.

Sexual abuse should always be reported, especially because silence protects and in a sense encourages the abuser to continue his or her activities. Abusers often bully their victims and instruct them to keep their activities a secret, often with the threat of punishment or even disgrace because, they claim, "No one will take your word against mine!"

What is the best action to take if you think that someone you know is being sexually abused?

It is probably wise to weigh the possible courses of action open to you. One option would be to discuss it with one or both of your parents. After urging them to regard this as a confidential matter, let them decide what is the wisest next step to take. Another option is to find the most trustworthy adult you know, preferably someone you have been able to confide in before and who knows you very well. This person may be a relative or teacher or counselor. It may seem safest to tell your best friend and hope that he or she will be able to help in some way, but you should remember that identifying and investigating a child abuser is an adult matter and for safety's sake should always be left to adults.

Of course, sexual abuse is against the law, and anyone who knows about a child or teenager who is being abused has an obligation to report that abuse to the proper authorities. For example, a police officer or doctor who takes care of a child or teenager who has been abused is obligated to investigate the matter and start legal action against the suspected abuser.

What is incest?

Incest is some type of sexual encounter or sexual abuse involving two members of the same family — father-daughter, mother-son, brother-sister, grandfather-granddaughter. It almost always is a male-female encounter involving blood relatives. Incest implies that the relationship is not between mutually consenting people — in other words, that some type of force or persuasion is involved. Sometimes no sign of force is apparent, but when a parent and child are involved, fear of exposure and fear of punishment have to be part of the relationship. The unspoken but acknowledged superior power and authority of the adult usually compel the child's agreement and cooperation. There may also be a desire on the part of the child or teenager to gain the attention and affection of the adult or sibling.

How can a person best seek protection from incest?

This probably is a matter of education. It is a subject that needs to be discussed, although it hardly ever is talked about in sex education classes at school or in Sunday school. Children as young as kindergarten age should know about both sexual abuse and incest. There are coloring books, role-playing games, television programs, and videotapes about abuse and incest in language and detail that are sensitive to specific age groups. During their formative years in school, children should be given as much age-appropriate information as they can absorb in nonthreatening, instructive ways. Undoubtedly, the best protection and prevention is education.

Parents should be especially sensitive to teenagers' increasing needs for personal modesty as they grow and mature. For example, both parents and adolescent children who walk around the house after taking a shower wearing only a towel, or who regularly cruise through the living room simply wearing underwear can be innocent, unintentional causes of sexual stimulation or arousal. Adults and near-adults should be conscious of and try to respect sensible boundaries of modesty.

If a parent or teenager feels uncomfortable or embarrassed by another family member's state of dress — or undress — he or she should speak up and say so, in a nonaccusatory, nonblaming way. Furthermore, as living space permits and other family members' needs are considered, teenagers should be given the privacy they feel they need. They certainly should have space to call their own and in which they can begin to define in privacy their individuality and personal lives.

What are the signs that indicate something more than proper or appropriate affection?

Parents should try to avoid inappropriate or excessive affectionate physical behavior with their teenagers: prolonged touching, feeling, kissing, hugging, tickling, squeezing, fondling, roughhousing, wrestling, spanking (especially fathers spanking daughters), tucking in or snuggling at bedtime, and similar activities that should have been outgrown.

There obviously is a line between kidding around and erotic (sexually arousing) behavior that parents and their adolescent children should be conscious of and try to avoid crossing. Clearly, the major burden of responsibility lies with parents to protect their teenagers from compromising, confusing, or embarrassing physical situations. On those comparatively few occasions when parents seem to have "lost it" — to be out of control or to have lost touch with their own sense of limits and boundaries — children should feel free to speak up and say, "Stop!" as forcefully as the situation permits.

In those even more rare situations when a parent refuses to stop — or stops and then starts again — the other parent must be prepared to step in. If the other parent is either unwilling, unable, or unavailable to take action, the child should seek help from an older sibling, a trusted relative, a trusted adult who knows the family, a teacher, a coach, or a counselor.

CHAPTER 18

SEX, ALCOHOL, AND DRUGS

Do drugs and alcohol have an effect on sex: sexual desire or level of arousal, performance, or inhibitions?

Drugs, including alcohol, are commonly thought to make a person feel sexually aroused, or "turned on," but, in reality, drugs actually interfere with or reduce sexual performance. Some males and females, in fact, may not be able to perform sexually while under the influence of drugs. Males may not be able to have or maintain an erection, and females may feel unable to respond to their partner's physical excitement.

Some individuals may find that a small amount of alcohol or some other drug will temporarily reduce worries, anxiety, or inhibitions (reluctance or unwillingness to engage in a particular action). Repeated or heavy use of any drug, however, will usually have a negative, unpleasant effect, which almost always makes sexual performance difficult or impossible.

Some prescription and over-the-counter drugs may interfere with sexual performance. Certain antihistamines, which may be taken to reduce allergic reactions, can cause drowsiness and may decrease sexual desire and ability to perform. Of course, any drug, either prescription or over-the-counter, taken in quantities greater than those described on the label or in the package, can have undesirable or unpredictable effects. If an over-the-counter drug appears to have an arousing effect upon a person's sexual desires, this may be the result of the individual's psychological expectation rather than a true drug response.

There is so much mythology and folklore associated with common street drugs, such as marijuana or cocaine, that many people expect a near-automatic "high." That simply does not happen. More often than not, when people use illegal drugs the effect is psychological — people say they feel a certain way because they want to feel that way. Most drugs, especially the well-known street drugs, reduce sexual capacity and performance. These drugs will not improve anyone's sex life or help with sexual problems. There is no single substance — drug, food, or beverage — that will provide a guaranteed sexual turn-on.

Does being drunk or on drugs have anything to do with the ability to conceive?

A female can conceive a child (get pregnant) just as easily while on drugs or when drunk on alcohol as when drug-free or sober. If the male has been taking drugs or drinking alcohol, he may not be able to maintain an erection and have sexual intercourse. If the female has intercourse while drunk or high, her ability to conceive remains unchanged, depending upon all the usual factors, including when intercourse occurs and the general condition of her health.

What is Spanish fly?

"Spanish fly" is the slang term for a very dangerous, highly irritating, even poisonous drug called cantharides. When applied to the female genitals, Spanish fly causes extreme irritation that might be misinterpreted as sexual excitement. If cantharides is given to a female it will not produce an uncontrollable urge or need to have sexual intercourse. It may, however, necessitate a trip to the doctor's office or a hospital emergency room for treatment because of the severe genital pain. Under no circumstances should anyone try to obtain or use Spanish fly, because the result can be very harmful.

What, if any, is the effect of the estrogen in marijuana on the male body?

There have been reports claiming that marijuana is responsible for breast enlargement in some teenage males who use that drug excessively. However, the evidence showing that this occurs is scanty at best. Whether estrogen is contained in marijuana in the first place remains a matter of debate.

Does estrogen in marijuana change the male sex hormones in any way?

Since we do not know if estrogen is present in significant amounts in marijuana in the first place, it is pointless to talk about male sex hormones being affected one way or another.

Does mixing a little saltpeter into food prevent males from having erections?

For generations, saltpeter (potassium nitrate) was thought to cut down sexual appetite, making it difficult for a male to have an erection. This belief has no scientific basis.

What is an aphrodisiac?

An aphrodisiac is any substance, usually a food or beverage, that is believed to increase sexual interest or heighten sexual appetite. The word comes from the name of the Greek goddess of love and beauty, Aphrodite.

What are a few types of aphrodisiacs?

Oysters, black olives, artichokes, and figs are a few examples of the many foods traditionally believed by some people to possess the capacity to stimulate human sexual appetite. The mere existence of the myth of aphrodisiacs illustrates the power of suggestion in the minds of people who would like to find a shortcut, so to speak, to sexual stimulation.

No one has ever produced evidence to support the claim that any of the so-called aphrodisiacs possesses properties or powers that have any effect on sexual feelings — or any other emotion, for that matter. However, as long as someone wants to connect success in sexual relations to what was eaten or drunk immediately before the sexual activity began, then the myth of aphrodisiacs having some kind of physical power will continue.

Can an aphrodisiac hurt a person in any way?

Unless consumed in very large quantities or over a prolonged period of time, aphrodisiac foods usually are not harmful to most people. If Spanish fly and other illicit drugs, however, are considered aphrodisiacs, then people should be aware that these substances are harmful and should not be used.

CHAPTER 19

INFERTILITY/STERILITY

What is sterility?

For a male, sterility means he cannot produce sperm, making it impossible for him to fertilize an egg and father a child. For a female, sterility means she cannot produce eggs, making it impossible for her to conceive a child.

Is sterility the same as infertility?

Sterility is not the same as infertility. A person who is sterile cannot father or conceive a child. An infertile individual has *reduced* ability to father or conceive a child. In the case of a female, it may be a problem with ovulation, and for the male, a problem with producing adequate sperm. Infertility can occur in both men and women, but it is not a "final event" as is sterility.

What kinds of problems cause sterility?

Sterility occurs in males and females for a variety of reasons. Infection can make a person sterile. The most common infections causing sterility are sexually transmitted diseases (STDs). Gonorrhea, syphilis, or chlamydia can produce sterility if not treated. (For more information, see Chapter 13, "Sexually Transmitted Diseases.")

For the female, an STD infection may block the fallopian tubes, and for the male, such an infection may block the vas deferens, the little canal that carries sperm to the urethra. The egg cannot go down the fallopian tubes, or sperm cannot get through the vas deferens into the urethra for release in an ejaculation. If these infections do not cause sterility, they may cause infertility when the passageways are partially blocked.

Radiation and chemotherapy (key-moe-THER-a-pee) can cause sterility. Cancer of the ovaries or testes often requires radiation treatment (the medical use of cell-destroying invisible rays given off by radioactive materials). Since cancer is life-threatening, doctors give radiation or chemotherapy (the use of powerful drugs), knowing that a side effect can be sterility. During even routine X-ray examinations, the reproductive organs are always shielded by lead aprons to prevent possible radiation damage.

There are a few rare genetic disorders, caused by abnormal chromosomes (the microscopic carriers of heredity in the cells), that cause a person to be sterile at birth. In addition, a severe injury to the testicles or vas deferens can make a man sterile.

Do some people choose to become sterile?

Yes, couples who have as many children as they want or can afford to raise often choose to become sterile. Surgical procedures that deliberately produce sterility include tube-tying for a woman and vasectomy for a man. Tube-tying means the fallopian tubes are cut and tied to prevent the egg from traveling into the uterus. Vasectomy means cutting the vas deferens to prevent sperm from entering the urethra. If couples later change their minds and decide that they want to have children, these operations are difficult to reverse.

If a man or woman is sterile, is it OK to have intercourse?

Of course it's all right for individuals who are sterile to have intercourse. No pregnancy can come of it. In addition, sterility rarely affects the pleasurable feelings associated with intercourse. People who are sterile, however, still need to take precautions against sexually transmitted diseases unless a couple has been together exclusively for years.

What's the difference between infertility and impotence?

Impotence is a male problem. It occurs when a male is unable to have or maintain an erection, which is a must for intercourse. As was said earlier, infertility is a reduced ability to produce sperm. An impotent male can be either fertile or infertile. (See Chapter

5, "Male Sexuality," and Chapter 8, "Hygiene, Health, and Medicine.")

Can infertility be caused by any of the following: heredity; an accident; an illness or disease; an active sex life; an excessive use of birth-control measures?

Infertility can be caused by heredity, that is, a male or female may inherit a tendency that makes it difficult to have children.

An accident that causes a severe groin injury can cause infertility in the male. Infertility and even sterility occur sometimes because of severing of both vas deferens in the groin area.

Infections, especially sexually transmitted diseases (STDs), can affect the female and male reproductive tracts, causing infertility until they are cured. Pelvic inflammatory disease (PID), for example, is an infection of the female reproductive system that can produce abdominal pain, often with fever. PID, caused by gonorrhea or chlamydia, often affects the fallopian tubes and can result in infertility or sterility. Other diseases of the female reproductive system also may cause infertility. A gynecologist (guy-na-COL-o-jist), a doctor who specializes in the care of the female reproductive system, usually diagnoses and treats infertility. (See Chapter 13, "Sexually Transmitted Diseases.")

Mumps is an infectious disease — not an STD — that can cause infertility, particularly in men.

Infertility can be caused by an active sex life *only* if the partner has an STD. Frequency of intercourse has little to do with infertility. If a male has intercourse three or four times over a period of, say, twelve hours, the last ejaculation may contain somewhat fewer sperm than the first, but his fertility is not lowered.

No evidence exists that the use of birth-control pills for any length of time can cause infertility. After discontinuing the birth-control pill, some females may not be able to become pregnant immediately, and they may blame their use of the pill for this failure. Using a diaphragm, condom, or foam is not associated with infertility. Infection may accompany the use of an IUD, and in rare cases this infection may cause infertility.

Does infertility occur often?

Accurate, meaningful statistical information on the incidence or frequency of infertility in the sexually active American population is difficult to obtain. Fertility problems are about as likely to occur with the male as with the female. It is estimated that one-third of the problems are related to the female, 30 to 40 percent are related to the male, and the rest result from a combination of male-female factors or have causes that cannot be pinpointed.

Is infertility contagious?

Infertility is not contagious. However, a male or female with an STD could pass the disease to a sexual partner. *No one with a sexually transmitted disease should engage in sexual activities until the disease is diagnosed, treated, and cured.*

How can people find out if they are infertile or sterile?

A female who cannot get pregnant after trying for a year should seek a fertility evaluation, and the male always needs to be included in this process. Both should consult a gynecologist and have a fertility evaluation, sometimes called a fertility work-up. Too often a female is made to feel that if she fails to conceive, it is her fault.

For the woman, a fertility work-up involves a routine vaginal exam to make sure that her reproductive organs are healthy. Lab tests of sample cells in the vagina and cervix are performed to check for infection. The quality of the cervical mucus is examined because if the mucus is very thick during the middle of the menstrual cycle, it may be difficult for sperm to penetrate the cervix. The acidity of the mucus also is checked; highly acid mucus can destroy sperm. If there is any question about the lining of the uterus, it may be necessary to take a tiny sample of tissue for examination under a microscope. This test, which can be done in a physician's office, is called a biopsy. It can show whether the tissue is normal for that time of the menstrual cycle. Other tests can show whether the fallopian tubes are clear. The health of the ovaries can be evaluated, sometimes with the aid of a laparoscope, a small, flexible, lighted telescope.

For the male, his semen is examined under a microscope to count the sperm; about 300 million to 500 million sperm per ejaculation is considered normal. In addition to number, the movement and shape of the sperm are observed. About 60 percent of the sperm should be in motion and look normal in size and shape.

As is obvious from this brief description, the female usually goes through more detailed examinations and evaluations than does the male. This difference reflects how complex the female reproductive system is.

What can be done about infertility?

If the cause of infertility in the female is blockage of the fallopian tubes, there are special kinds of surgery that can attempt to reopen the tubes. A laparoscope — a kind of miniature telescope — is inserted into the abdomen through a very small incision under the navel. The physician attempts to reopen the blocked tube. A male may be infertile because of a physical abnormality, usually present from birth, in his reproductive system that interferes with the delivery of sperm. Some types of physical abnormalities can be corrected by surgery.

Suppose both partners have a fertility work-up and are found to be normal and still cannot conceive. Can anything else be done to overcome infertility?

Other physical and psychological factors have to be considered. For the female, keeping track of her ovulation times can be helpful. For example, she can record her temperature daily, and by noting its variations she and her doctor can determine exactly when she ovulates. Couples trying to conceive usually become very body- and time-conscious. For example, they may want to have intercourse, if possible, at precisely the "right time" of each month to coincide with ovulation. They may run into "scheduling difficulties," but where there's a will, there's often a way! The stress created by the situation itself and, possibly, by other psychological factors needs to be faced and discussed. Sometimes couples try very hard to conceive, and it just doesn't happen. Occasionally, childless couples who finally adopt a child find that the wife becomes pregnant, perhaps because the pressure they lived with while trying to conceive has vanished.

What can be done to overcome sterility?

If the male is sterile, pregnancy is impossible except by getting a suitable male to donate sperm. If a female is sterile, pregnancy is impossible except by finding a substitute mother or, in some cases, by trying an alternative technique to attempt to conceive.

What are some alternative methods of conception if a couple, for whatever reason, cannot conceive?

Several methods now exist to promote conception. First is *artificial insemination,* the oldest and perhaps simplest alternative way to achieve a pregnancy. This method is used if a couple is unable to conceive because one or both partners are infertile or if a single or divorced female wishes to have a child. Sperm is obtained by having the male masturbate. The sperm is then placed directly into the female's vagina, through a syringe, by a doctor or team of doctors specializing in human reproduction.

If the male partner is sterile, a couple may choose, with a doctor's assistance, to obtain sperm from a donor. A doctor can transfer the sperm via artificial insemination to the female.

The sperm may come from one of the "sperm banks" located in several major medical centers in the United States specializing in the science of human reproduction. A sperm bank is simply a laboratory where sperm is collected, classified according to physical and family traits of the donors, and stored. The sperm is frozen for later use in artificial insemination and other methods of assisting human conception. When scientifically stored in a modern laboratory, frozen sperm and eggs can last three or more years.

There is a method called *self-donation of sperm.* Suppose, for example, that a male becomes ill and needs treatment that might make him sterile. For cancer, the treatment might be radiation, or for other diseases, powerful drugs that often reduce sperm production. Before treatment begins, the man might want to place his sperm in a sperm bank where it could be frozen for use later if needed in the event medical treatment made him infertile or sterile.

In vitro fertilization (meaning "in glass" — specifically, in a laboratory culture dish) involves removing eggs from the ovary of a woman whose fallopian tubes may be blocked. The eggs are placed in a culture dish and mixed with sperm from her partner, or from a donor if her partner is sterile. The fertilized egg (or eggs) is permitted to divide just a few times while doctors observe it continuously under a microscope. Then they return the developing egg to the woman's body. They implant it directly and carefully in the wall of the uterus, which they reach through the vagina and the cervix. If the attempt works, the female becomes pregnant. Doctors almost always implant more than one fertilized egg at a time in the wall of the uterus because of the difficulty of getting even one to stay in place and grow. Occasionally, more than one fertilized egg survives, and so the woman has two (or more) babies. The entire in vitro fertilization process is extremely delicate and expensive, and about one out of four attempts succeeds.

For a woman who is unable to have a child, finding a *surrogate (substitute) mother* may be an option. For instance, a woman might be unable to carry a child because of a condition called endometriosis (end-o-meet-tree-oh-sis), where the lining of her uterus cannot accept and hold the fertilized egg. Or she might have a chronic disease, such as diabetes or emphysema, which could make a pregnancy harmful to her health or life. The surrogate mother has the couple's fertilized egg implanted in her uterus by an "in vitro" medical team. She then carries and delivers the baby. After birth, the baby is given to the mother and father as previously agreed.

If a woman has lost her ovaries through disease or surgery, there may be two options. First, she might have a donated egg from another woman, fertilized by in vitro fertilization, implanted in her own sound uterus. She would then carry the donated egg through pregnancy. Or she might be able to engage a surrogate mother who would, in effect, donate her own egg for artificial insemination with the woman's partner's sperm, or with donated sperm if the partner is sterile. The surrogate mother would be carrying her own fertilized egg through the pregnancy. After birth, the baby would be given to the couple who made the agreement with her.

A recently developed method of artificially assisted conception is called *gamete intrafallopian transfer* (GIFT). The doctor removes several eggs from the woman's ovary and mixes them with the partner's sperm. The mixture is placed in the woman's fallopian tube, where fertilization may occur. The hope is that implantation of the fertilized egg in the uterus could occur naturally without medical assistance.

abortion — the interruption, or termination, of a pregnancy. This can be either by spontaneous abortion, also called miscarriage, or an induced abortion, which is a surgical procedure.

AIDS (acquired immune deficiency syndrome) — a contagious infectious disease caused by a human immunodeficiency virus, or HIV. The virus attacks special white blood cells that help fight infection, and as a result, the body develops unusual severe infections.

AIDS-related complex (ARC) — a less severe form of AIDS. Symptoms include fever, diarrhea, weight loss, and night sweats. About 25 percent of people with ARC develop AIDS within three years.

aphrodisiac — any substance, usually a food or beverage, that is believed to increase sexual interest or heighten sexual appetite.

artificial insemination — a method of conception in which donated sperm is injected into a female's vagina.

Bartholin's glands — two small glands in the female reproductive system that secrete mucus that helps lubricate the vagina.

birth control — measures used to prevent pregnancy; also called contraception.

blue balls — a slang term referring to the color of the swollen blood vessels in the scrotum.

cervical cap — a rubber contraceptive device that is inserted into the vagina to cover the cervix and prevent sperm from entering the uterus.

cervix — the entrance to the uterus and fallopian tubes. It extends down into the top of the vagina.

chlamydia — the most common sexually transmitted disease. Symptoms include discomfort and difficulty in urinating for the male, and vaginal discharge and abdominal discomfort for the female.

circumcision — the surgical removal of the foreskin, which naturally covers the head of the penis. Circumcision is usually performed within the first few days after a male is born.

climacteric — also called the midlife crisis. A time in life, usually in the forties or fifties, when hormone levels decrease, possibly causing depression. For females, this is the same as menopause.

clitoris — a small bump in the genital area of females that is a major source of sexual sensitivity.

coitus interruptus — an unreliable method of birth control where a male withdraws his penis from the female's vagina before ejaculation occurs. This is also called withdrawal.

conception — the moment when pregnancy begins, when the fertilized egg becomes implanted in the uterus.

condom — a very thin sheath that fits over the erect penis to prevent pregnancy by keeping sperm from entering the female's vagina. Condoms also protect against sexually transmitted diseases.

contraception — the science and methods involved with preventing pregnancy. Also referred to as birth control.

Cowper's glands — pea-sized structures in the male reproductive system located near the urethra that contribute some of the fluid that makes up the semen a male ejaculates.

cunnilingus — oral sex involving kissing, licking, or sucking the female's vulva, clitoris, and vagina.

D and C (dilation and curettage) — a method of cleaning out the uterus that involves enlarging the cervix and then gently scraping the uterus lining.

DES (diethylstilbestrol) — a synthetic female hormone that was used in the 1950s to prevent miscarriage and other pregnancy-related disorders. Daughters of women who took DES have a higher risk of cancer of the vagina and cervix.

dildo — an object shaped like an erect penis that is used to create sexual stimulation and excitement.

diaphragm — a contraceptive device in the form of a flexible ring that is covered with rubber and fits over the female's cervix to prevent sperm from entering the uterus.

douche — a fluid used to clean and flush out the vagina.

ejaculation — the spurting release of semen, sperm-containing fluid, from the erect penis at the peak or climax of sexual excitement.

endometriosis — a medical condition that causes a female to be unable to carry a baby because the lining of her uterus cannot accept and hold the fertilized egg.

erectile tissue — specialized human tissue that becomes hard or rigid during sexual excitement or through friction. Erectile tissue is present in the male penis and female and male nipples.

erogenous zone — a part or region of the body that is especially sensitive to sexual excitement because of the large number of nerve endings located there. The genital region in males and females, for example, is an erogenous zone.

estrogen — a female hormone responsible for triggering much of female sexual development.

fallopian tubes — narrow channels leading from the ovaries to the uterus. The fallopian tubes carry eggs from the ovaries down toward the uterus during the menstrual cycle.

fellatio — oral stimulation of the penis by kissing, licking, or sucking.

fertile — capable of reproducing: for human beings this means being able to become pregnant or to bring about pregnancy.

fetus — the name given to the developing baby carried in the female uterus during pregnancy.

fimbria — the tiny, fingerlike projection of tissue at the top of the fallopian tubes that reaches out and wraps around each ovary.

foreplay — the process through which humans become sexually aroused by kissing, necking, and petting.

fraternal twins — two babies developing in the same uterus that result from two eggs, each of which is fertilized by separate sperm. They can be of the same sex or one female and one male.

genital herpes — a lifelong sexually transmitted disease, caused by a virus, that produces painful blisters on the shaft of the penis or in the vagina.

genitals — the male and female external sex organs that are fully or partially visible. The genital area refers to the place at the bottom of the abdomen and between the legs.

GIFT (gamete intrafallopian transfer) — a method of artificially assisted conception involving the mixing of eggs and sperm in a laboratory. The mixture is then placed in a female's fallopian tube, where fertilization may occur, followed by implantation in the uterus.

glans — the rounded tip of the penis, also called the head.

gonads — the male sex glands, also called testicles or balls.

gonorrhea — a common sexually transmitted disease caused by *n. gonococci* bacteria.

gynecologic exam — the medical examination of a female's external and internal reproductive organs.

hermaphrodite — a term meaning "part male, part female," referring to those individuals born with genital organs and other characteristics of both sexes.

heterosexual — a male or a female who is attracted to individuals of the opposite sex over a significant period of time.

homosexual — a male or a female who is attracted to individuals of the same sex over a significant period of time.

hormone — a complex chemical that certain organs (such as ovaries or testicles) or glands (such as the thyroid or pituitary) produce and release into the bloodstream. Certain hormones trigger changes in sexual organs and are responsible for maintaining healthy reproductive organs.

horny — the slang term used to describe someone who is sexually aroused or lustful, or who desires sexual stimulation.

hot flash — a feeling of sudden intense warmth accompanied by sweating. Females who are going through menopause sometimes experience hot flashes.

hymen — the thin layer of tissue stretching across a female's vagina near its lower opening.

hysterectomy — an operation involving the surgical removal of a female's uterus. It may also involve removal of part or all of the ovaries.

identical twins — two babies that develop after one egg is fertilized by one sperm and the egg divides in such a way that two separate embryos develop. These cells can grow into twins of the same sex, sharing identical sets of genetic material.

immune system — various blood cells, especially the white cells, involved in defending the body against infectious organisms.

impotence — a condition, either temporary or long-term, affecting a male in such a way that he cannot have or maintain an erection.

infertility — reduced ability to either conceive or father a child.

intercourse — the sexual joining of two individuals; also called having sex or making love.

intrauterine device (IUD) — a contraceptive device in the form of a small, specially designed object that a physician inserts into a female's uterus.

in vitro fertilization — an alternative method of conception involving the removal of eggs from a female's ovary, their fertilization with sperm in a laboratory, and then implantation of the fertilized egg(s) in her uterus.

labia — the visible part of the vaginal area. Labia means "lips" of the vagina.

libido — instinctive sexual behavior or sexual desire, sometimes called the sex drive.

masturbation — stimulating the genital organs, usually with the hand, without engaging in sexual intercourse.

menopause — that time of life, lasting from one to five years, when a female's menstrual cycle gradually ceases. Sometimes called the change of life.

menstrual cycle — the complete chain of events, from the beginning of one menstrual flow to the beginning of the next, usually lasting 28 to 30 days.

menstrual period — the time during which a female is menstruating.

menstruation — the monthly shedding of a female's uterus lining, which is made of blood and tissue.

miscarriage — a pregnancy that does not continue following the fertilization of an egg. Also known as a spontaneous abortion.

mons — the pad of soft, fatty tissue that covers the pubic bone in the lowest part of a female's abdomen.

mucus method — a system of physical observation sometimes used by females who are trying to get pregnant. By checking the changing thickness of her cervical mucus over the course of a month, a female can estimate when she is ovulating, that is, when she is fertile and likely to become pregnant.

oral herpes — an infection of the mouth and lips that produces cold sores or fever blisters. The virus that causes oral herpes is related to the virus that causes genital herpes.

orgasm — the peak or climax of sexual excitement. For the female, it is vigorous contraction of the vaginal muscles and uterus. For the male, it is ejaculation of semen from the erect penis.

ovaries — two almond-sized organs that produce eggs for release in sexually mature females during the menstrual cycle.

ovulation — the process of releasing an egg from the ovaries each month.

oral sex — using the mouth to stimulate the genital area of the sexual partner.

Pap smear — a simple, routine medical procedure to collect some of the cells lining the cervix for later microscopic examination.

pelvic inflammatory disease (PID) — severe, persistent abdominal pain in females, often accompanied by fever, caused by a sexually transmitted disease.

penis — the male sexual organ, consisting of the head and the shaft.

petting — sexual stimulation by feeling and stroking the partner's body, including the arms, chest, breasts, legs, and perhaps the genitals, either outside or inside the clothes.

the pill (birth-control pill) — a prescription drug used by females to prevent pregnancy.

pornography — writing, pictures, television, or any other form of communication intended to excite sexual desire.

premenstrual syndrome (PMS) — the regular occurrence of certain physical and psychological problems before menstruation begins or in the early days of a female's period.

progesterone — a hormone produced when fertilization does not occur. Progesterone is needed to stop menstrual bleeding.

prolactin — a hormone that causes nipple discharge, including lactation in women who are breast-feeding.

prophylactic — a device designed to prevent conception and the spread of sexually transmitted diseases. A condom, or rubber, is a type of prophylactic.

prostate gland — a small, circular gland located behind the scrotum that supplies 30 to 40 percent of the fluid in a male's semen.

puberty — the time of rapid physical development when sexual reproduction first becomes possible for human beings.

pubic — refers to the genital area where the sex organs are located. Thick, wiry hair called pubic hair grows in this region.

reproductive system — a group of related organs in the human body that perform sexual activities and conceive and give birth.

rhythm method — a method of birth control that involves refraining from sexual intercourse during the time of ovulation.

sado-masochism — sexual activity that involves giving and receiving punishment, both physical and psychological.

scabies — a skin disease, caused by a tiny insect called a mite, that may be associated with sexually transmitted disease.

scrotum — the flexible bag of skin that holds the testicles.

semen — the sperm-containing fluid ejaculated from the erect penis during the peak of sexual excitement.

seminal vesicles — two small, coiled-up tubes, located behind the scrotum, that produce fluid for the semen.

sex drive — instinctive sexual behavior or activity.

sexual intercourse — the sexual joining of two individuals; also may be called having sex or making love.

sexually transmitted disease (STD) — the preferred term for a variety of diseases that are spread through intimate sexual contact. Also called venereal disease.

Spanish fly — the slang term for a very dangerous, highly irritating, even poisonous drug called cantharides.

sperm — the male sex cells necessary for fertilization of a female's eggs.

sperm bank — a laboratory where sperm is collected, classified, and stored for research and used for human conception.

sterility — for a male, sterility means that he cannot produce sperm; for a female, sterility means that she cannot produce eggs.

sterilization — a surgical procedure that makes a male or female unable to start a pregnancy.

surrogate mother — a female who contracts to accept a couple's fertilized egg, carry the baby through pregnancy, and then deliver it. The newborn is given to the couple, who pays the surrogate (substitute) mother for her services.

syphilis — a sexually transmitted disease caused by an infection that produces a painless, ulcerated sore, called a chancre, usually on the shaft of the penis or in the vagina.

temperature method — a procedure used by females who are trying to get pregnant, which involves keeping track of temperature to determine the days when it is slightly elevated, indicating ovulation.

testicles — the male sex glands, also called testes or gonads, that create sperm in sexually mature males in response to testosterone.

testosterone — the male sex hormone that is responsible for stimulating male sexual development.

transsexual — the term used to describe a person who has undergone a sex change operation in order to assume the physical characteristics and identity of the opposite sex.

transvestite — a person who dresses and tries to behave like someone of the opposite sex.

tubal ligation — female sterilization. Cutting or sealing off the fallopian tubes to prevent pregnancy; also called having one's tubes tied.

urethra — the canal, or tube, leading from the bladder that carries urine out of the body.

uterus — the small, muscular organ in a female's abdominal region that carries the developing fetus during pregnancy. The uterus is also called the womb.

vagina — the genital canal that extends from the uterus to the vulva. It is the opening for sexual intercourse, the passage for menstrual flow to be carried out of the body, and the birth canal.

vas deferens — the two slim tubes, sometimes called sperm ducts, that carry sperm from the testicles to the seminal vesicles for storage until ejaculation.

vasectomy — male sterilization. The surgical cutting and sealing off of the vas deferens to prevent sperm from being ejaculated.

venereal disease (VD) — a popular name for any sexually transmitted disease.

vulva — the covering of the female's external reproductive area. The vulva includes the pubic hair, the labia, and the entire genital area.

wet dreams — ejaculation of semen during the night, sometimes accompanied by sexually stimulating dreams. Technically known as nocturnal emissions, wet dreams are normal and occur most often during early and middle adolescence.

withdrawal method — the practice used by a male when he removes his erect penis from the female's vagina before ejaculation occurs. Also known as coitus interruptus.

womb — the small, muscular organ located in a female's lower abdominal region, also known as the uterus, that carries the developing fetus during pregnancy.

X chromosome — one of the two types of genetic material that determine the sex of human beings. Two X chromosomes produce a female.

Y chromosome — one of the two types of genetic material that determine the sex of human beings. An X and a Y chromosome produce a male.

yeast infection — a common fungus infection that can affect males and females. Yeast infections, which can be spread by sexual intercourse, cause itching and irritation along with either vaginal discharge or an inflamed penis.

INDEX